PEARL

A New Verse Translation

by

Rebekah Curry

Acknowledgment is made to the editors of *The Evansville Review*, in which sections I-III of this translation first appeared.

Cover design by Rebekah Curry. Cover image by Piotr Szczepanski/Shutterstock.com.

ISBN 979-8-218-78578-9

Table of Contents

Translator's Preface

The poem known as *Pearl* was written sometime in the late fourteenth century. It has been preserved in the manuscript designated Cotton Nero A.x., which is now held by the British Library. In the same manuscript, following *Pearl*, are three other long poems presumably by the same author: *Patience* and *Cleanness*, both didactic works based on biblical narratives, and the Arthurian poem *Sir Gawain and the Green Knight*. The author's identity is unknown; from the historical and literary context, he is assumed to have been male, and he is commonly referred to either as the Pearl Poet or the Gawain Poet. Some scholars have proposed, largely on the basis of alleged cryptograms and acrostics contained in the texts, that he was a man named John or Hugh Massey, but this idea is far from universally accepted. What can be said with certainty is that the poet was well educated, knowledgeable about both literature and theology, as well as courtly manners and the life of the nobility, which provides so much of the background for both *Pearl* and *Sir Gawain*. He also was interested and greatly skilled in the use of complex poetic forms.

Pearl falls under the medieval genre of the dream vision, in which the dreamer learns some religious or moral truth, often with the help of an enlightened guide who leads him or her on a symbolic journey. At the beginning of the poem, the unnamed narrator is in mourning for his "pearl," which was lost in a garden and lies underground in decay. He sinks into a dream and finds himself in a landscape of unearthly beauty. Traversing it, he comes to a river and sees on the opposite bank a queenly maiden, whom he realizes is known to him. When he expresses grief for his loss of her, she rebukes him, telling him to accept the will of God. He inquires as to the nature of her life in the heavenly kingdom, and the two begin a dialogue as she asserts, over his objections, that all the citizens of heaven have royal honors regardless of their earthly age or status. Abashed by her wisdom and authority, the narrator finally ceases to question her but asks that he be allowed to see where she dwells. He is granted a sight of the divine city, the New Jerusalem. Upon seeing the Pearl-Maiden walking there with her companions, he is overwhelmed by his desire to be reunited with her and leaps into the river, intending to swim across. However, at that moment he awakens. Although saddened to be separated from her again, he resolves to love and submit to God just as she has.

The most common interpretation of *Pearl* is that the poem is a father's elegy for his daughter who died in infancy. This is never explicitly stated in the text. However, the narrator says that the Pearl-Maiden lived "not two years" on earth and that she was "nearer to [him] than aunt or niece." The latter reference, along with the manner in which the two interact, has led many to conclude that they are parent and child. Others suggest that *Pearl* is more likely to have been a memorial of bereavement suffered by the poet's patron or an allegory in which the pearl represents, for example, the purity of the soul. The question of whether the poet and the narrator are the same person, or whether the poem is "true," is debatable. Yet even if it is not grounded in the poet's personal experience, the relationship of the narrator to the Pearl-Maiden is believably portrayed. Throughout the poem, the narrator's sadness clouds his mind as he struggles to accept the doctrines that she expounds. He loves her and rejoices to see her glorified but, perhaps still thinking of her as a child, finds it difficult to believe that her knowledge is greater than his own. The lessons that she teaches are not immediately applied; even at the end of the poem, as he repents of his self-will and impatience, it remains for him to fully come to terms with his situation.

The form of *Pearl* is unique and elaborate. The poem is made up of twenty sections, each of which contains five stanzas, with the exception of the fifteenth section, which has six. Each stanza has twelve lines rhyming *ababababbcbc*. The meter has four stresses per line, and these stressed syllables frequently alliterate, although not according to any strict pattern. The stanzas within a section are connected by the device of concatenation; each one is built around a "link-word" that recurs in both the first and last line:

> Since in that *spot* it sprang from me,
> I often long for that nonpareil
> that once made every sorrow flee
> and gave fair fortune and life as well.
> This yearning pierces me painfully,
> seizes my heart, makes it burn and swell.
> I never thought that a song could be
> so sweet as the one that gently fell
> in stillness, as I was grieved to tell
> her shape was marred with a dirty clot.
> O earth, you deface a lovely belle,
> my precious pearl without a *spot*.
>
> With herbs that *spot* must be overspread,
> …

The poem comes full circle, as the link-word of the final section appears at the end of the very first line. In this way, the overall structure imitates the perfect circular form of the pearl. The only inconsistency is the extra stanza in the fifteenth section, which causes the total to add up to 101 stanzas instead of 100; significantly, 101 is also the stanza count of *Sir Gawain*. With its twelve-line stanzas, *Pearl* is thus 1,212 lines long, and this is important in terms of numeric symbolism. The foundation of the New Jerusalem has twelve levels, and its dimensions are said in the poem to be twelve by twelve furlongs; the numbers of the 144,000 virgins and the twenty-four elders are further multiples. In some biblical interpretations, twelve is considered to be a sacred number, that of the twelve apostles and tribes of Israel, and the poet no doubt had this in mind.

The language of *Pearl* is Middle English of the Northwest Midlands dialect. It is far less intelligible to a modern audience than is the London dialect used by the Pearl Poet's contemporary Geoffrey Chaucer in *The Canterbury Tales*, even if a partially modernized spelling convention is adopted, eliminating archaic letters such as thorn (þ) and yogh (ȝ). Thus, a Modern English rendition is required to make the poem accessible to the majority of readers. In translating *Pearl*, my first concern was to preserve the metrical and rhyme schemes in an effort to communicate the experience of reading the original. Except when dealing with certain link-words, I made the decision to use exact rhymes rather than slant or sight rhymes, in order to maintain the cohesion of the stanzaic structure. I also determined that I would retain the original rhymes as often as possible, even when the poet sometimes uses a word more than once in a stanza or a rhyme sound more than once in a section. I tried to alliterate as the opportunity arose. Finally, in terms of vocabulary, I allowed a certain number of rare and obsolete words, particularly in the service of rhyme, but consciously avoided archaic pronouns and verb forms (e.g., *Thou giv'st*) except when rendering biblical quotations.

A project of this complexity could hardly be completed without some assistance. I am grateful to TEAMS, the Teaching Association for Medieval Studies, which, in association with the University of Rochester and Western Michigan University, publishes the Middle English Texts Series. In making this translation, I frequently consulted their edition of *Pearl*, edited by Sarah Stanbury. The Middle English text included in this book is that made available through the University of Michigan Library Digital Collections in their *Corpus of Middle English Prose and Verse*. Many thanks are due to Willis Barnstone, who selected sections I through III of this translation for the 2016 Willis Barnstone Translation Prize, and to the editors of *The Evansville Review*, where that excerpt was published. Stanley Lombardo's interest and encouragement were greatly appreciated. Likewise, as in all my other endeavors, my parents had nothing but words of support. And in the end, of course, I am indebted to the poet himself, that "gentyl jueler."

Rebekah Curry
March 2025

PEARL

A New Verse Translation

I

Pearl, that a prince in pleasure's way
displays in settings of gold so clear;
in all the Orient, I daresay,
I never came on her priceless peer.
So round, so lovely in each array,
so smooth, with her shape a perfect sphere;
wherever I judged that gems were gay,
I set her apart on the highest tier.
Alas, in a garden I lost my dear;
she tumbled away in a grassy plot.   10
With lovelorn longing my eyes are blear,
for that precious pearl without a spot.

Since in that spot it sprang from me,
I often long for that nonpareil
that once made every sorrow flee
and gave fair fortune and life as well.
This yearning pierces me painfully,
seizes my heart, makes it burn and swell.
I never thought that a song could be
so sweet as the one that gently fell   20
in stillness, as I was grieved to tell
her shape was marred with a dirty clot.
O earth, you deface a lovely belle,
my precious pearl without a spot.

With herbs that spot must be overspread
where such rich soil to rot is run;
there blossoms of white and blue and red
all shine so gaily against the sun.
No flower or fruit could be witherèd
with its roots in leafmould dark and dun.   30
Grain must grow from seeds that are dead,
or those who harvest could gather none.
From good each good thing is begun;
from seeds so lovely is beauty got,
or spice-plants springing would not be won
from that precious pearl without a spot.

I

Perle, pleasaunte to prynces paye
To clanly clos in golde so clere,
Oute of oryent, I hardyly saye,
Ne proued I neuer her precios pere.
So rounde, so reken in vche araye,
So smal, so smoþe her sydeȝ were,
Quere-so-euer I jugged gemmeȝ gaye,
I sette hyr sengeley in synglere.
Allas! I leste hyr in on erbere;
Þurȝ gresse to grounde hit fro me yot.   10
I dewyne, fordolked of luf-daungere
Of þat pryuy perle wythouten spot.

Syþen in þat spote hit fro me sprange,
Ofte haf I wayted, wyschande þat wele,
Þat wont watȝ whyle deuoyde my wrange
And heuen my happe and al my hele.
Þat dotȝ bot þrych my hert þrange,
My breste in bale bot bolne and bele;
Ȝet þoȝt me neuer so swete a sange
As stylle stounde let to me stele.   20
For soþe þer fleten to me fele,
To þenke hir color so clad in clot.
O moul, þou marreȝ a myry iuele,
My priuy perle wythouten spotte.

Þat spot of spyseȝ mot nedeȝ sprede,
Þer such rycheȝ to rot is runne;
Blomeȝ blayke and blwe and rede
Þer schyneȝ ful schyr agayn þe sunne.
Flor and fryte may not be fede
Þer hit doun drof in moldeȝ dunne;   30
For vch gresse mot grow of grayneȝ dede;
No whete were elleȝ to woneȝ wonne.
Of goud vche goude is ay bygonne;
So semly a sede moȝt fayly not,
Þat spryngande spyceȝ vp ne sponne
Of þat precios perle wythouten spotte.

To the spot that I speak of in my rhyme
I went one day in that garden green,
in the month of August, at Lammas-time
when grain is cut with sickles keen. 40
Where my pearl was lost, bright flowers climb
the hill and lighten it with their sheen;
ginger and gillyvor in their prime
and peonies growing in between.
As fair to my sight I found this scene,
there flowed a fragrance more fair, I wot.
I know my treasure there lies serene,
my precious pearl without a spot.

Before that spot with hands in fold
I stood as in care my heart was caught. 50
So deep within me grief lay cold,
yet patience was what my reason taught.
I mourned for my pearl hid under mould,
as doubts and desires fiercely fought;
woe had my wretched will in hold,
though Christ was a comfort to my thought.
The airs such drowsy sweetness brought,
I sank upon that flowery plot,
and wandering in a sleep I sought
that precious pearl without a spot. 60

II

From that spot my spirit sprang in space;
my body lay asleep and blind.
My soul was gone, by God's good grace,
in quest where men may marvels find.
I knew not what to call that place
but saw the cliffs that rose behind.
Toward a forest then I turned my face,
where rocks gleamed, of the richest kind.
None would believe the light that shined,
their radiant glory was so rare; 70
no tapestry that one designed
could ever be adorned so fair.

To þat spot þat I in speche expoun
I entred in þat erber grene,
In Auguste in a hyȝ seysoun,
Quen corne is coruen wyth crokeȝ kene.   40
On huyle þer perle hit trendeled doun
Schadowed þis worteȝ ful schyre and schene,
Gilofre, gyngure and gromylyoun,
And pyonys powdered ay bytwene.
Ȝif hit watȝ semly on to sene,
A fayr reflayr ȝet fro hit flot.
Þer wonys þat worþyly, I wot and wene,
My precious perle wythouten spot.

Bifore þat spot my honde I spenned
For care ful colde þat to me caȝt;   50
A deuely dele in my hert denned,
Þaȝ resoun sette myseluen saȝt.
I playned my perle þat þer watȝ spenned
Wyth fyrce skylleȝ þat faste faȝt;
Þaȝ kynde of Kryst me comfort kenned,
My wreched wylle in wo ay wraȝte.
I felle vpon þat floury flaȝt,
Suche odour to my herneȝ schot;
I slode vpon a slepyng-slaȝte
On þat precios perle wythouten spot.   60

II

Fro spot my spyryt þer sprang in space;
My body on balke þer bod in sweuen.
My goste is gon in Godeȝ grace
In auenture þer meruayleȝ meuen.
I ne wyste in þis worlde quere þat hit wace,
Bot I knew me keste þer klyfeȝ cleuen;
Towarde a foreste I bere þe face,
Where rych rokkeȝ wer to dyscreuen.
Þe lyȝt of hem myȝt no mon leuen,
Þe glemande glory þat of hem glent;   70
For wern neuer webbeȝ þat wyȝeȝ weuen
Of half so dere adubbemente.

4

So fair adorned those hillsides lay
with crystal clear in hue as snow,
and all about a woodland way
with trees as blue as indigo.
The leaves like burnished silver play
on quivering branches where they grow;
beneath the sky's unclouded ray
they shine most brightly, all aglow. 80
The pebbles on the ground below
were precious pearls beyond compare.
So pale and dim the sunbeams show
in light of that adornment fair.

Those hillsides' fair adornment made
my spirit lay all grief aside.
Such fragrant fruits grew in that glade,
by scent alone I was satisfied.
With plumages of every shade,
birds flew together in their pride; 90
citole or gittern that one played
could never match how sweet they cried.
For as those birds went winging wide,
their music's roundel filled the air.
No other joy could stand beside
the sight of that adornment fair.

Thus fair adorned was all I found
in that wood where fortune guided me.
No mortal tongue could once expound
upon its splendor fittingly. 100
I went unhindered over ground,
as full of bliss as one might be.
The farther wood, the fairer crowned
with spices and fruits and greenery,
and riverbanks and lovely lea;
like gold the streamlets glistened there.
I reached a river running free—
Lord, its adornment was so fair!

Dubbed wern alle þo downeȝ sydeȝ
Wyth crystal klyffeȝ so cler of kynde.
Holtewodeȝ bryȝt aboute hem bydeȝ
Of bolleȝ as blwe as ble of Ynde;
As bornyst syluer þe lef on slydeȝ,
Þat þike con trylle on vch a tynde.
Quen glem of glodeȝ agaynȝ hem glydeȝ,
Wyth schymeryng schene ful schrylle þay schynde.   80
Þe grauayl þat on grounde con grynde
Wern precious perleȝ of oryente:
Þe sunnebemeȝ bot blo and blynde
In respecte of þat adubbement.

The adubbemente of þo downeȝ dere
Garten my goste al greffe forȝete.
So frech flauoreȝ of fryteȝ were,
As fode hit con me fayre refete.
Fowleȝ þer flowen in fryth in fere,
Of flaumbande hweȝ, boþe smale and grete;   90
Bot sytole-stryng and gyternere
Her reken myrþe moȝt not retrete;
For quen þose bryddeȝ her wyngeȝ bete,
Þay songen wyth a swete asent.
So gracios gle couþe no mon gete
As here and se her adubbement.

So al watȝ dubbet on dere asyse
Þat fryth þer fortwne forth me fereȝ.
Þat derþe þerof for to deuyse
Nis no wyȝ worþé þat tonge bereȝ.   100
I welke ay forth in wely wyse;
No bonk so byg þat did me dereȝ.
Þe fyrre in þe fryth, þe feier con ryse
Þe playn, þe plontteȝ, þe spyse, þe
And raweȝ and randeȝ and rych reuereȝ,
As fyldor fyn her bonkes brent.
I wan to a water by schore þat schereȝ —
Lorde, dere watȝ hit adubbement!

The fair adornments of that stream
were banks that shone with beryl bright.   110
Its sweeping currents sweetly seem
to murmur flowing in their flight.
Within those depths, rich jewels gleam
as if through sunlit glass, as right
as stars, when folk take rest and dream,
stare from the sky in winter night.
The stones that came into my sight
were emerald, sapphire, scattered where
the pool's waters brimmed with light,
for its adornment was so fair.   120

III

The fair adornment of down and dale,
of wood and water and lovely plains,
built up my joy, made sorrow fail,
banished distress and vanquished pains.
I followed a river through the vale,
as bliss would overwhelm my brains;
the farther I went along its trail,
more strength of joy within me strains.
As fortune over mankind reigns
to give them solace or grieving sore,   130
the one who has what she ordains
will come to have still more and more.

More happiness than I could say,
though time allow, was in that state;
no earthly spirit ever may
grasp but a tenth of joy so great.
Over the riverbanks' broad way,
I thought that Paradise must wait,
but deep the flood before me lay.
I guessed the water was a gate   140
between delights, to separate
a country with higher bliss in store.
I dared not wade across the spate,
and ever I longed still more and more.

The dubbemente of þo derworth depe
Wern bonke3 bene of beryl bry3t.   110
Swangeande swete þe water con swepe,
Wyth a rownande rourde raykande ary3t.
In þe founce þer stonden stone3 stepe,
As glente þur3 glas þat glowed and gly3t,
As stremande sterne3, quen stroþe-men slepe,
Staren in welkyn in wynter ny3t;
For vche a pobbel in pole þer py3t
Wat3 emerad, saffer, oþer gemme gente,
Þat alle þe lo3e lemed of ly3t,
So dere wat3 hit adubbement.   120

III

The dubbement dere of doun and dale3,
Of wod and water and wlonk playne3,
Bylde in me blys, abated my bale3,
Fordidden my stresse, dystryed my payne3.
Doun after a strem þat dry3ly hale3
I bowed in blys, bredful my brayne3;
Þe fyrre I fol3ed þose floty vale3,
Þe more strenghþe of ioye myn herte strayne3.
As fortune fares þer as ho frayne3,
Wheþer solace ho sende oþer elle3 sore,   130
Þe wy3 to wham her wylle ho wayne3
Hytte3 to haue ay more and more.

More of wele wat3 in þat wyse
Þen I cowþe telle þa3 I tom hade,
For vrþely herte my3t not suffyse
To þe tenþe dole of þo gladne3 glade;
Forþy I þo3t þat Paradyse
Wat3 þer ouer gayn þo bonke3 brade.
I hoped þe water were a deuyse
Bytwene myrþe3 by mere3 made;   140
By3onde þe broke, by slente oþer slade,
I hoped þat mote merked wore.
Bot þe water wat3 depe, I dorst not wade,
And euer me longed ay more and more.

More and more and yet more again
I wished to see the other side,
although that land was lovely, when
the farther was more beautified.
I stopped and looked about me then
to find a ford, and long I tried,   150
but the peril grew more great, I ken,
the farther I went along that tide.
And ever I thought I should not bide
in fear with such delights before.
But a new wonder I espied
that moved my mind still more and more.

More marvels then amazed my mind;
I saw beyond that water where
a cliff of crystal brightly shined;
its rays resplendent rose aflare.   160
And at the foot of it was shrined
a child of gentle grace so rare,
in gleaming robes of wondrous kind.
I knew her, I had seen her ere.
As gold refined is pure and fair,
so was the maid upon that shore.
At length I looked upon her there;
the longer, I knew her more and more.

The more that I surveyed her face,
her figure, and her royal dress,   170
such gladness gave to me its grace
as little before I might possess.
I longed to call to her apace,
but awe had struck me with distress.
To see her in so strange a place,
it held my heart in hard duress.
She raised her head; her loveliness,
the shining visage that she wore,
so dazed me, I may not express
my wonderment, the more and more.   180

More and more, and ȝet wel mare,
Me lyste to se þe broke byȝonde;
For if hit watȝ fayr þer I con fare,
Wel loueloker watȝ þe fyrre londe.
Abowte me con I stote and stare;
To fynde a forþe faste con I fonde. 150
Bot woþeȝ mo iwysse þer ware,
Þe fyrre I stalked by þe stronde.
And euer me þoȝt I schulde not wonde
For wo þer weleȝ so wynne wore.
Þenne nwe note me com on honde
Þat meued my mynde ay more and more.

More meruayle con my dom adaunt:
I seȝ byȝonde þat myry mere
A crystal clyffe ful relusaunt;
Mony ryal ray con fro hit rere. 160
At þe fote þerof þer sete a faunt,
A mayden of menske, ful debonere;
Blysnande whyt watȝ hyr bleaunt.
I knew hyr wel, I hade sen hyr ere.
As glysnande golde þat man con schere,
So schon þat schene an-vnder shore.
On lenghe I loked to hyr þere;
Þe lenger, I knew hyr more and more.

The more I frayste hyr fayre face,
Her fygure fyn quen I had fonte, 170
Suche gladande glory con to me glace
As lyttel byfore þerto watȝ wonte.
To calle hyr lyste con me enchace,
Bot baysment gef myn hert a brunt.
I seȝ hyr in so strange a place,
Such a burre myȝt make myn herte blunt.
Þenne vereȝ ho vp her fayre frcount,
Hyr vysayge whyt as playn yuore:
Þat stonge myn hert ful stray atount,
And euer þe lenger, þe more and more. 180

IV

More than I wished, my dread grew vast.
I stood stock-still and dared not call;
with staring eyes and lips sealed fast,
I stayed as a hunting hawk in hall.
I thought she had a ghostly cast,
and thus I feared what might befall
if, as I looked, the vision passed
ere I could make her stop or stall.
So gracious, with no flaw in all,
she rose up in her vesture bright, 190
so soft and sweetly slight, so small,
a precious thing with pearls bedight.

Bedight with pearls of royal fee,
one might by fortune's grace have seen
her there, as fresh as fleur-de-lis,
come quickly down that bank so green.
Her robes were white as ivory
and decked as would befit a queen
with the choicest pearls, it seems to me,
that I had looked on, all pristine. 200
Her trailing sleeves, I wot and ween,
were trimmed with pearls in double plight,
her kirtle of the selfsame sheen,
with precious pearls so well bedight.

Bedight was the crown upon that girl
with pearls and still no other stone,
high pinnacles of perfect pearl
and filigrees like flowers grown.
No coif or wimple close did furl
the hair about her shoulders thrown. 210
She looked as grave as duke or earl,
her countenance more white than bone.
Her locks that were so loosely strown
lay like spun gold in lustrous light.
Her broidered collar too was sewn
with precious pearls and rich bedight.

IV

More þen me lyste my drede aros.
I stod ful stylle and dorste not calle;
Wyth yȝen open and mouth ful clos
I stod as hende as hawk in halle.
I hoped þat gostly watȝ þat porpose;
I dred onende quat schulde byfalle,
Lest ho me eschaped þat I þer chos,
Er I at steuen hir moȝt stalle.
Þat gracios gay wythouten galle,
So smoþe, so smal, so seme slyȝt,
Ryseȝ vp in hir araye ryalle,
A precios pyece in perleȝ pyȝt.   190

Perleȝ pyȝte of ryal prys
Þere moȝt mon by grace haf sene,
Quen þat frech as flor-de-lys
Doun þe bonke con boȝe bydene.
Al blysnande whyt watȝ hir beau biys,
Vpon at sydeȝ, and bounden bene
Wyth þe myryeste margarys, at my deuyse,
Þat euer I seȝ ȝet with myn ene;   200
Wyth lappeȝ large, I wot and I wene,
Dubbed with double perle and dyȝte;
Her cortel of self sute schene,
Wyth precios perleȝ al vmbepyȝte.

A pyȝt coroune ȝet wer þat gyrle
Of mariorys and non oþer ston.
Hiȝe pynakled of cler quyt perle,
Wyth flurted flowreȝ perfet vpon.
To hed hade ho non oþer werle;
Her here leke, al hyr vmbegon,   210
Her semblaunt sade for doc oþer erle,
Her ble more blaȝt þen whalleȝ bon.
As schorne golde schyr her fax þenne schon,
On schyldereȝ þat leghe vnlapped lyȝte.
Her depe colour ȝet wonted non
Of precios perle in porfyl pyȝte.

Bedight was the hem and broidered wide
at her wrists, her sides, each aperture,
with white pearls and no gem beside,
and brilliant white her garments were. 220
A pearl that had no flaw to hide
upon her breast was set secure;
one's mind would be left stupefied
ere he might take its measure sure.
I think no tongue could once endure
to find words fitting for that sight,
it was so clean and clear and pure,
the precious pearl that her bedight.

Bedight with pearls, that precious piece
came down upon the grassy floor; 230
no gladder man from here to Greece
than I was as she stood on shore.
She was nearer to me than aunt or niece;
therefore my joy was much the more.
She bowed to me and did not cease
to speak as suits a woman's lore,
took off the coronet she wore
and gave me greeting glad and light.
Well was it I was born afore
to answer that sweet with pearls bedight! 240

V

"O pearl," said I, "with pearls bedight,
are you my pearl that I have plained
and grieved for all alone by night?
Much longing I have hid restrained
since you went gleaming in your flight.
With sorrow I am sorely pained,
while you live daily in delight,
in Paradise, by strife unstrained.
My jewel, what fate has thus ordained
that I must mourn without you here? 250
For since the two of us were twained,
I have been a joyless jeweler."

Pyȝt watȝ poyned and vche a hemme
At honde, at sydeȝ, at ouerture,
Wyth whyte perle and non oþer gemme,
And bornyste quyte watȝ hyr uesture.   220
Bot a wonder perle wythouten wemme
Inmyddeȝ hyr breste watȝ sette so sure;
A manneȝ dom moȝt dryȝly demme,
Er mynde moȝt malte in hit mesure.
I hope no tong moȝt endure
No sauerly saghe say of þat syȝt,
So watȝ hit clene and cler and pure,
Þat precios perle þer hit watȝ pyȝt.

Pyȝt in perle, þat precios pyece
On wyþer half water com doun þe schore.   230
No gladder gome heþen into Grece
Þen I, quen ho on brymme wore.
Ho watȝ me nerre þen aunte or nece;
My joy forþy watȝ much þe more.
Ho profered me speche, þat special spece,
Enclynande lowe in wommon lore,
Caȝte of her coroun of grete tresore
And haylsed me wyth a lote lyȝte.
Wel watȝ me þat euer I watȝ bore
To sware þat swete in perleȝ pyȝte!   240

V

'O perle', quod I, 'in perleȝ pyȝt,
Art þou my perle þat I haf playned,
Regretted by myn one on nyȝte?
Much longeyng haf I for þe layned,
Syþen into gresse þou me aglyȝte.
Pensyf, payred, I am forpayned,
And þou in a lyf of lykyng lyȝte,
In Paradys erde, of stryf vnstrayned.
What wyrde hatȝ hyder my iuel vayned,
And don me in þys del and gret daunger?   250
Fro we in twynne wern towen and twayned,
I haf ben a joyleȝ juelere.'

That jewel then, with gems besprent,
raised up her face with eyes of grey,
put on her pearls of Orient,
and solemnly began to say,
"Sir, you have erred in argument
to say your pearl has gone away,
that as in a casket comely pent
lies in this gracious garden gay,   260
herein forevermore to stay,
where mourning never may come near.
Here would your treasure be, in fay,
if you were a gentle jeweler.

"But, jeweler, if you suppose
your gem is gone that you held lief,
you are the author of your woes,
to trouble with a thing so brief.
For what you lost was but a rose
that flowered and fell in nature's fief.   270
Now in the chest its keeper chose,
it proves a pearl of price most chief.
And you have called your fate a thief,
which brought this forth from naught, 'tis clear;
you blame the remedy for your grief.
You are an unkind jeweler."

A jewel to me was this guest,
and jewels the gentle words she said.
"Indeed," said I, "of maidens best,
because of you, distress has fled.   280
To be excused I make request;
I thought my pearl was perishèd.
I will rejoice that I am blessed
to dwell where its dear light is shed,
and love my Lord as He has led
me where bright bliss is always near.
If I could cross this riverbed,
I would be a joyful jeweler."

15

That juel þenne in gemmeȝ gente
Vered vp her vyse wyth yȝen graye,
Set on hyr coroun of perle orient,
And soberly after þenne con ho say:
'Sir, ȝe haf your tale mysetente,
To say your perle is al awaye,
Þat is in cofer so comly clente
As in þis gardyn gracios gaye,   260
Hereinne to lenge for euer and play,
Þer mys nee mornyng com neuer nere.
Her were a forser for þe, in faye,
If þou were a gentyl jueler.

'Bot, jueler gente, if þou schal lose
Þy ioy for a gemme þat þe watȝ lef,
Me þynk þe put in a mad porpose,
And busyeȝ þe aboute a raysoun bref;
For þat þou lesteȝ watȝ bot a rose
Þat flowred and fayled as kynde hyt gef.   270
Now þurȝ kynde of þe kyste þat hyt con close
To a perle of prys hit is put in pref.
And þou hatȝ called þy wyrde a þef,
Þat oȝt of noȝt hatȝ mad þe cler;
Þou blameȝ þe bote of þy meschef,
Þou art no kynde jueler.'

A juel to me þen watȝ þys geste,
And iueleȝ wern hyr gentyl saweȝ.
'Iwyse', quod I, 'my blysfol beste,
My grete dystresse þou al todraweȝ.   280
To be excused I make requeste;
I trawed my perle don out of daweȝ.
Now haf I fonde hyt, I schal ma feste,
And wony wyth hyt in schyr wod-schaweȝ,
And loue my Lorde and al his laweȝ
Þat hatȝ me broȝt þys blys ner.
Now were I at yow byȝonde þise waweȝ,
I were a ioyful jueler.'

"Jeweler," said that gem so clean,
"why will you jest thus foolishly?   290
You have said three words at once, I ween;
unwise, in truth, are all these three.
You have no thought of what they mean;
your words before your wits do flee.
You think me in this valley green
because your eyes my image see.
Another—you say that you will be
where I am, to stay with me here.
The third—to cross this water free.
That may no joyful jeweler.   300

VI

"I give that jeweler little praise
who loves well what he sees with eye,
and much of blame the one betrays
who thinks our Lord would make a lie,
who truly promised your life to raise
though fate had doomed your flesh to die.
You only love what meets your gaze
and set His every word awry.
No good man must be tempted by
this thought that is a proof of pride—   310
to let no tale be true to try
but what his own mind may decide.

"Decide now if your speech has been
such as is fit that God receive.
You say that you will dwell herein;
I say you ought to first ask leave,
and yet might fail such grant to win.
You wish this passage to achieve;
that cannot be, because of sin.
Your corpse to earth must coldly cleave;   320
our father Adam and his Eve
condemned it in the dust to bide.
In dire death a man must grieve
ere he may cross as God decide."

'Jueler', sayde þat gemme clene,
'Wy borde ȝe men? So madde ȝe be!
Þre wordeȝ hatȝ þou spoken at ene:
Vnavysed, for soþe, wern alle þre.
Þou ne woste in worlde quat on dotȝ mene;
Þy worde byfore þy wytte con fle.
Þou says þou traweȝ me in þis dene,
Bycawse þou may wyth yȝen me se;
Anoþer þou says, in þys countré
Þyself schal won wyth me ryȝt here;
Þe þrydde, to passe þys water fre —
Þat may no ioyfol jueler. 300

VI

'I halde þat iueler lyttel to prayse
Þat leueȝ wel þat he seȝ wyth yȝe,
And much to blame and vncortayse
Þat leueȝ oure Lorde wolde make a lyȝe,
Þat lelly hyȝte your lyf to rayse,
Þaȝ fortune dyd your flesch to dyȝe.
Ȝe setten hys wordeȝ ful westernays
Þat leueȝ noþynk bot ȝe hit syȝe.
And þat is a poynt o sorquydryȝe,
Þat vche god mon may euel byseme, 310
To leue no tale be true to tryȝe
Bot þat hys one skyl may dem.

'Deme now þyself if þou con dayly
As man to God wordeȝ schulde heue.
Þou saytȝ þou schal won in þis bayly;
Me þynk þe burde fyrst aske leue,
And ȝet of graunt þou myȝteȝ fayle.
Þou wylneȝ ouer þys water to weue;
Er moste þou ceuer to oþer counsayle:
Þy corse in clot mot calder keue. 320
For hit watȝ forgarte at Paradys greue;
Oure ȝorefader hit con misseȝeme.
Þurȝ drwry deth boȝ vch man dreue,
Er ouer þys dam hym Dryȝtyn deme.'

"If you decide," I said, "my dear,
to cast me hence, I can but plain.
At last I find my jewel here—
shall we be torn again in twain?
Why must I lose what stands so near?
My precious pearl gives me great pain.   330
What does treasure bring but grief and tear
to one who gathers it in vain?
I care not if I lose all gain,
nor if I must be banished wide;
without my pearl that has no stain,
awaiting woe I must decide."

"You decide to stay in your distress,"
then said that one. "Why do you so?
In mourning over what is less,
a man must often the more forgo.   340
You would do better yourself to bless
and love God ever in weal and woe,
for anger gives you no redress.
Who suffers should not stubborn show,
for though you writhe as wounded doe
and struggle against what pains betide,
when still you may no further go,
endure what doom He shall decide.

"Decide that the Lord does wrong to you;
He will move not a foot from off His way.   350
Though sorrow fills your heart with rue,
there is small worth in what you say.
Now cease complaint, contention too,
and seek His pardon as well you may.
Your prayer may pierce His pity through,
that mercy will its might display.
His comfort may drive your grief away,
so all your sorrows soon subside;
for though you lament and murmur aye,
all lies with Him to alone decide."   360

'Deme3 þou me', quod I, 'my swete,
To dol agayn, þenne I dowyne.
Now haf I fonte þat I forlete,
Schal I efte forgo hit er euer I fyne?
Why schal I hit boþe mysse and mete?
My precios perle dot3 me gret pyne.
What serue3 tresor, bot gare3 men grete
When he hit schal efte wyth tene3 tyne?
Now rech I neuer for to declyne,
Ne how fer of folde þat man me fleme.
When I am partle3 of perle myne,
Bot durande doel what may men deme?'

'Thow deme3 no3t bot doel-dystresse',
Þenne sayde þat wy3t. 'Why dot3 þou so?
For dyne of doel of lure3 lesse
Ofte mony mon forgos þe mo.
Þe o3te better þyseluen blesse,
And loue ay God, in wele and wo,
For anger gayne3 þe not a cresse.
Who nede3 schal þole, be not so þro.
For þo3 þou daunce as any do,
Braundysch and bray þy braþe3 breme,
When þou no fyrre may, to ne fro,
Þou moste abyde þat he schal deme.

'Deme Dry3tyn, euer hym adyte,
Of þe way a fote ne wyl he wryþe.
Þy mende3 mounte3 not a myte,
Þa3 þou for sor3e be neuer blyþe.
Stynt of þy strot and fyne to flyte,
And sech hys blyþe ful swefte and swyþe.
Þy prayer may hys pyté byte,
Þat mercy schal hyr crafte3 kyþe.
Hys comforte may þy langour lyþe
And þy lure3 of ly3tly fleme;
For, marre oþer madde, morne and myþe,
Al lys in hym to dy3t and deme.'

330

340

350

360

VII

I decided to say to that damozel,
"Now let me not my Lord offend
if rashly I in speech rebel.
Such pain of loss my heart did rend,
as spilling water springs from well.
I hope His mercy may descend.
Do not rebuke me that I fell,
though I do wrong and must amend,
but kindly to me your comfort send,
with pity when you think of this: 370
you have made grief to be my friend,
who were ever the ground of all my bliss.

"My bliss you were and yet my bane,
for so much greater was my care
when you disappeared from earth's domain.
My pearl was gone, I knew not where.
Now I see that which soothes my pain.
We parted as a perfect pair;
God forbid that in strife we strain.
so seldom we meet, either here or there.   380
Though in courtesy you speak me fair,
I am but dust and manners miss.
But Christ's mercy, Mary, and John I bear
to be the ground of all my bliss.

"By bliss I see you blithely lit,
and I a man whom sorrows sate;
yet you take little note of it,
though often I suffer grief so great.
But now that I see you where you sit,
I would beseech, without debate,   390
that you say, as sober words befit,
what life you lead both early and late.
For I am glad of your estate,
as one of worthiness now it is;
to all my joy the highway gate,
it is at the ground of all my bliss."

VII

Thenne demed I to þat damyselle:
'Ne worþe no wrathþe vnto my Lorde,
If rapely I raue, spornande in spelle.
My herte watȝ al wyth mysse remorde,
As wallande water gotȝ out of welle.
I do me ay in hys myserecorde.
Rebuke me neuer wyth wordeȝ felle,
Þaȝ I forloyne, my dere endorde,
Bot kyþeȝ me kyndely your coumforde,
Pytosly þenkande vpon þysse: 370
Of care and me ȝe made acorde,
Þat er watȝ grounde of alle my blysse.

'My blysse, my bale, ȝe han ben boþe,
Bot much þe bygger ȝet watȝ my mon;
Fro þou watȝ wroken fro vch a woþe,
I wyste neuer quere my perle watȝ gon.
Now I hit se, now leþeȝ my loþe.
And, quen we departed, we wern at on;
God forbede we be now wroþe,
We meten so selden by stok oþer ston.   380
Þaȝ cortaysly ȝe carp con,
I am bot mol and manereȝ mysse.
Bot Crystes mersy and Mary and Jon,
Þise arn þe grounde of alle my blisse.

'In blysse I se þe blyþely blent,
And I a man al mornyf mate;
ȝe take þeron ful lyttel tente,
Þaȝ I hente ofte harmeȝ hate.
Bot now I am here in your presente,
I wolde bysech, wythouten debate,   390
ȝe wolde me say in sobre asente
What lyf ȝe lede erly and late.
For I am ful fayn þat your astate
Is worþen to worschyp and wele, iwysse;
Of alle my joy þe hyȝe gate,
Hit is in grounde of alle my blysse.'

"Now bliss, man, may you well betide,"
she said, whose loveliness has no peer;
"you are welcome here to walk and bide,
for your speech is pleasant to my ear.   400
Masterful mood and lofty pride,
I assure you, are hotly hated here.
My Lord does not delight to chide,
for meek are all that He holds near,
and when before Him you shall appear,
be devout in meekness such as this.
To my Lord the Lamb such is always dear;
that is the ground of all my bliss.

"Of blissful life you say I tell;
you wish to measure its degree.   410
You know at the time that your pearl fell
I was so tender in infancy,
but my Lord, whose godhead must excel,
in His marriage has enfolded me,
crowned me a queen in bliss to dwell
through length of days that shall ever be.
His inheritance is given free
to her He loves. I am wholly His—
His precious prize, and His royalty
is root and ground of all my bliss."   420

VIII

"O blissful," I said, "may this be true?
Your pardon if in speech I stray.
Are you the queen of heavens blue,
to whom the world must homage pay?
We believe in Mary from whom grace grew,
who was a mother and yet a may.
To take her crown—who might so do
but to surpass her in some way?
For the sweetness she can alone display,
we call her the Phoenix of Araby,   430
which flawless flew in her bright array,
like to the Queen of courtesy."

'Now blysse, burne, mot þe bytyde',
Þen sayde þat lufsoum of lyth and lere,
'And welcum here to walk and byde,
For now þe speche is to me dere.   400
Maysterful mod and hy3e pryde,
I hete þe, arn heterly hated here.
My Lorde ne loue3 not for to chyde,
For meke arn alle þat wone3 hym nere;
And when in hys place þou schal apere,
Be dep deuote in hol mekenesse.
My Lorde þe Lamb loue3 ay such chere,
Þat is þe grounde of alle my blysse.

'A blysful lyf þou says I lede;
Þou wolde3 knaw þerof þe stage.   410
Þow wost wel when þy perle con schede
I wat3 ful 3ong and tender of age;
Bot my Lorde þe Lombe þur3 hys godhede,
He toke myself to hys maryage,
Corounde me quene in blysse to brede
In lenghe of daye3 þat euer schal wage;
And sesed in alle hys herytage
Hys lef is. I am holy hysse:
Hys prese, hys prys, and hys parage
Is rote and grounde of alle my blysse.'   420

VIII

'Blysful', quod I, 'may þys be trwe?
Dysplese3 not if I speke errour.
Art þou þe quene of heuene3 blwe,
Þat al þys worlde schal do honour?
We leuen on Marye þat grace of grewe,
Þat ber a barne of vyrgyn flour;
Þe croune fro hyr quo mo3t remwe
Bot ho hir passed in sum fauour?
Now, for synglerty o hyr dousour,
We calle hyr Fenyx of Arraby,   430
Þat freles fle3e of hyr fasor,
Lyk to þe Quen of cortaysye.'

"Courteous Queen," that fair one prayed,
kneeling and lifting up her face,
"Matchless Mother, most joyous Maid,
blessed beginner of each grace!"
Then she rose up, for a moment stayed,
but returned in her speech to me apace:
"Many seek reward and are well repaid,
but usurpers may not dwell in this space.   440
She has all heaven in her embrace
with earth and hell in her empery,
yet no other heir will she displace,
for she is the Queen of courtesy.

"The court of the kingdom of God alive
is of this nature in fashioning:
each one who may therein arrive
of all the realm is queen or king,
yet never the others shall deprive,
but is glad they possess so great a thing   450
and would wish their crowns more rich by five,
if 'twere possible for their bettering.
But my lady of whom Jesu did spring
over us all has sovereignty;
none thinks it overmastering,
for she is the Queen of courtesy.

"Of courtesy, so says Saint Paul,
as members of Christ we may be seen;
as head and arm and leg must all
be faithfully joined to Him, I ween,   460
each Christian soul has this same call,
to belong to our Lord in His demesne.
Think, then, if hatred or any gall
can tie itself your limbs between.
Your head can have no spite or spleen
at the hand adorned with jewelry.
So we behave to king and queen,
with joy and love, by courtesy."

'Cortayse Quen', þenne sayde þat gaye,
Knelande to grounde, folde vp hyr face,
'Makeleȝ Moder and myryest May,
Blessed bygynner of vch a grace!'
Þenne ros ho vp and con restay,
And speke me towarde in þat space:
'Sir, fele here porchaseȝ and fongeȝ pray,
Bot supplantoreȝ none wythinne þys place.   440
Þat emperise al heuenȝ hatȝ,
And vrþe and helle, in her bayly;
Of erytage ȝet non wyl ho chace,
For ho is Quen of cortaysye.

'The court of þe kyndom of God alyue
Hatȝ a property in hytself beyng:
Alle þat may þerinne aryue
Of alle þe reme is quen oþer kyng,
And neuer oþer ȝet schal depryue,
Bot vchon fayn of oþereȝ hafyng,   450
And wolde her corouneȝ wern worþe þo fyue,
If possyble were her mendyng.
Bot my Lady of quom Jesu con spryng,
Ho haldeȝ þe empyre ouer vus ful hyȝe;
And þat dyspleseȝ non of oure gyng,
For ho is Quene of cortaysye.

'Of courtaysye, as saytȝ Saynt Poule,
Al arn we membreȝ of Jesu Kryst:
As heued and arme and legg and naule
Temen to hys body ful trwe and tryste,   460
Ryȝt so is vch a Krysten sawle
A longande lym to þe Mayster of myste.
Þenne loke what hate oþer any gawle
Is tached oþer tyȝed þy lymmeȝ bytwyste.
Þy heued hatȝ nauþer greme ne gryste,
On arme oþer fynger þaȝ þou ber byȝe.
So fare we alle wyth luf and lyste
To kyng and quene by cortaysye.'

"In courtesy I do believe;
in charity you all delight.   470
But as you hear me, do not grieve;
I think that you speak not aright.
In youth such queenship to receive—
you raise yourself too far in height.
What honor more could one achieve
who had endured the world's long night
in lifelong penance, that he might
thus purchase bliss with agony?
Who is more worthy to be dight
with a kingly crown by courtesy?   480

IX

"That courtesy does all bounds exceed,
if 'tis such as you say to me.
You were not two years with us, indeed;
how to please God you could not see,
knew not the Pater nor the Creed—
and made a queen so hastily!
I cannot think, so God me speed,
He would be unjust in His decree.
Now a countess in this realm to be,
it would befit you, by my fay,   490
or else a lady of less degree—
but to be queen from that first day!"

"On no day may His goodness be constrained,"
then said to me that worthy wight,
"for all is truth that He ordained,
and He may do naught but what is right.
In Matthew's message is contained,
in the gospel of the God of might,
a parable that He well explained
and likened to His kingdom bright.   500
Said He, 'My realm on heaven's height
is like a vinery that lay
when the time to tend it was in sight;
its lord knew the appointed day.'

27

'Cortaysé', quod I, 'I leue,
And charyté grete, be yow among,   470
Bot my speche þat yow ne greue,
. . . .
Þyself in heuen ouer hyȝ þou heue,
To make þe quen þat watȝ so ȝonge.
What more honour moȝte he acheue
Þat hade endured in worlde stronge,
And lyued in penaunce hys lyueȝ longe
Wyth bodyly bale hym blysse to byye?
What more worschyp moȝt he fonge
Þen corounde be kyng by cortaysé?   480

IX

'That cortaysé is to fre of dede,
Ȝyf hyt be soth þat þou coneȝ saye.
Þou lyfed not two ȝer in oure þede;
Þou cowþeȝ neuer God nauþer plese ne pray,
Ne neuer nawþer Pater ne Crede;
And quen mad on þe fyrst day!
I may not traw, so God me spede,
Þat God wolde wryþe so wrange away.
Of countes, damysel, par ma fay,
Wer fayr in heuen to halde asstate,   490
Oþer elleȝ a lady of lasse aray;
Bot a quene! Hit is to dere a date.'

'Þer is no date of hys godnesse',
Þen sayde to me þat worþy wyȝte,
'For al is trawþe þat he con dresse,
And he may do noþynk bot ryȝt.
As Mathew meleȝ in your messe
In sothfol gospel of God almyȝt,
In sample he can ful grayþely gesse,
And lykneȝ hit to heuen lyȝte.   500
"My regne", he saytȝ, "is lyk on hyȝt
To a lorde þat hade a uyne, I wate.
Of tyme of ȝere þe terme watȝ tyȝt,
To labor vyne watȝ dere þe date.

"Of that day in spring all knew the sign.
Early that morn the lord arose
to hire workmen for his vine,
and some to his purposes he chose.
They made their contract then; in fine,
for a penny a day they work the rows   510
of terraces where the grape-stems twine,
prune them and bind them as each grows.
Later the lord to market goes
and sees men idling as they stay.
'Why stand you idle?' he said to those.
'Do you not know the time of day?'

"'Ere day had dawned, we had begun
to seek some work, and long we sought.
We have stood here since rise of sun,
but no man bids us to do aught.'   520
'Go to my vineyard, every one,'
the lord said, and their labor bought.
'Whatever wage by night is run
I pledge to pay, withholding naught.'
So to the task they turned their thought,
and so the lord went on his way
and new men to his vineyard brought,
almost until the close of day.

"When the day had waned to evensong,
an hour before the sun would set,   530
he saw men idling, young and strong,
and said to every one he met,
'Why stand you idle for so long?'
They answered, 'None has hired us yet.'
'Go with my workmen, join their throng,
and honest wages you will get.'
Soon the skies grew black as jet;
he went to the vineyard then to pay
the laborers his stated debt,
for it was late, and done the day.   540

'"Þat date of ȝere wel knawe þys hyne.
Þe lorde ful erly vp he ros
To hyre werkmen to hys vyne,
And fyndeȝ þer summe to hys porpos.
Into acorde þay con declyne
For a pené on a day, and forth þay gotȝ,
Wryþen and worchen and don gret pyne,
Keruen and caggen and man hit clos.
Aboute vnder þe lorde to marked totȝ,
And ydel men stande he fyndeȝ þerate.
'Why stande ȝe ydel?' he sayde to þos.
'Ne knawe ȝe of þis day no date?'

'""Er date of daye hider arn we wonne',
So watȝ al samen her answar soȝt.
'We haf standen her syn ros þe sunne,
And no mon byddeȝ vus do ryȝt noȝt.'
'Gos into my vyne, dotȝ þat ȝe conne',
So sayde þe lorde, and made hit toȝt.
'What resonabele hyre be naȝt be runne
I yow pay in dede and þoȝte.'
Þay wente into þe vyne and wroȝte,
And al day þe lorde þus ȝede his gate,
And nw men to hys vyne he broȝte
Welneȝ wyl day watȝ passed date.

'"At þe date of day of euensonge,
On oure byfore þe sonne go doun,
He seȝ þer ydel men ful stronge
And sade to hem wyth sobre soun,
'Wy stonde ȝe ydel þise dayeȝ longe?'
Þay sayden her hyre watȝ nawhere boun.
'Gotȝ to my vyne, ȝemen ȝonge,
And wyrkeȝ and dotȝ þat at ȝe moun.'
Sone þe worlde bycom wel broun;
Þe sunne watȝ doun and hit wex late.
To take her hyre he mad sumoun;
Þe day watȝ al apassed date.

510

520

530

540

X

"The time of day the lord did know;
'Foreman,' he called, 'come, bring their fee!
Pay them the hire that I owe,
and further, so none finds fault with me,
set all of them along a row
and give each a penny equally.
Begin with the last man that stands low,
so on to the first you oversee.'
The first complained he was too free
and said that they had toiled sore: 550
'These worked a single hour! So we
think that we ought to take the more.

"'More we deserve, so we declare,
who have endured the daylong heat,
which they for not two hours did bear—
and yet the same reward you mete.'
Said the lord to one who murmured there,
'Friend, none do I wish to cheat.
I hired you for a penny fair;
go hence and take your due receipt.   560
Whom will you say that I ill-treat?
Was a penny not contracted for?
Our settlement is all complete.
Why then will you ask for more?

"'More, is it not my lawful right
to keep my own, to give it too?
Or is your eye thus turned to spite,
that I cheated neither them nor you?'
'Thus shall,' said Christ, 'I each requite;
the last shall be the first, and who   570
was first the last, though swift his flight.
Those called are many; those chosen, few.'
So poor men ever receive their due,
though they came late and little bore;
though little from their works accrue,
the mercy of God is much the more.

X

'"The date of þe daye þe lorde con knaw,
Called to þe reue: 'Lede, pay þe meyny.
Gyf hem þe hyre þat I hem owe,
And fyrre, þat non me may reprené,
Set hem alle vpon a rawe
And gyf vchon inlyche a peny.
Bygyn at þe laste þat standeȝ lowe,
Tyl to þe fyrst þat þou atteny.'
And þenne þe fyrst bygonne to pleny
And sayden þat þay hade trauayled sore:
'Þese bot on oure hem con streny;
Vus þynk vus oȝe to take more.

'""More haf we serued, vus þynk so,
Þat suffred han þe dayeȝ hete,
Þenn þyse þat wroȝt not houreȝ two,
And þou dotȝ hem vus to counterfete.'
Þenne sayde þe lorde to on of þo:
'Frende, no waning I wyl þe ȝete;
Take þat is þyn owne, and go.
And I hyred þe for a peny agrete,
Quy bygynneȝ þou now to þrete?
Watȝ not a pené þy couenaunt þore?
Fyrre þen couenaunde is noȝt to plete.
Wy schalte þou þenne ask more?

'""More, weþer louyly is me my gyfte,
To do wyth myn quat-so me lykeȝ?
Oþer elleȝ þyn yȝe to lyþer is lyfte
For I am goude and non byswykeȝ?'
Þus schal I", quod Kryste, "hit skyfte:
Þe laste schal be þe fyrst þat strykeȝ,
And þe fyrst þe laste, be he neuer so swyft;
For mony ben called, þaȝ fewe be mykeȝ."
Þus pore men her part ay pykeȝ,
Þaȝ þay com late and lyttel wore;
And þaȝ her sweng wyth lyttel atslykeȝ,
Þe merci of God is much þe more.

550

560

570

"More have I of joy and bliss herein,
of life's fair bloom and ladyship's pride,
than all the ones in the world might win
if they made what claims were justified.   580
Although but lately I did begin
and came to the vine at eventide,
in mind of my hire my Lord had been;
at once my wages were set aside.
Yet others labored and long did bide,
who added nothing to their score
although in toil and sweat they plied—
for years they might receive no more."

Then more I spoke and plainly said:
"God's right and power may not fail.   590
No reason is in the speech you sped,
or Holy Writ is but a tale.
A verse in the Psalter may be read,
too clear for doubt to ever assail:
'Thou giv'st what reward is merited,
Thou king on high whom all must hail.'
Another endured the day's travail,
and yet in payment you came before.
So the less are weighed on a greater scale;
the longer that they do less, the more."   600

XI

"Between more and less no doubt is laid,"
she said, "in the kingdom of our Lord,
for there in full each man is paid,
whether little or much be his reward.
Our gentle Sovereign has never stayed
whatever of hard or soft He stored;
as waters from a dike cascade
or currents rush, so His gifts are poured.
His goodness is abundant toward
the one He saves from sin and woe;   610
no blessings will be withheld in hoard,
for the grace of God is great enow.

'More haf I of joye and blysse hereinne,
Of ladyschyp gret and lyueȝ blom,
Þen alle þe wyȝeȝ in þe worlde myȝt wynne
By þe way of ryȝt to aske dome.   580
Wheþer welnygh now I con bygynne —
In euentyde into þe vyne I come —
Fyrst of my hyre my Lorde con mynne:
I watȝ payed anon of al and sum.
Ȝet oþer þer werne þat toke more tom,
Þat swange and swat for long ȝore,
Þat ȝet of hyre noþynk þay nom,
Paraunter noȝt schal to-ȝere more.'

Then more I meled and sayde apert:
'Me þynk þy tale vnresounable.   590
Goddeȝ ryȝt is redy and euermore rert,
Oþer Holy Wryt is bot a fable.
In Sauter is sayd a verce ouerte
Þat spekeȝ a poynt determynable:
"Þou quyteȝ vchon as hys desserte,
Þou hyȝe kyng ay pretermynable."
Now he þat stod þe long day stable,
And þou to payment com hym byfore,
Þenne þe lasse in werke to take more able,
And euer þe lenger þe lasse, þe more.'   600

XI

'Of more and lasse in Godeȝ ryche',
Þat gentyl sayde, 'lys no joparde,
For þer is vch mon payed inlyche,
Wheþer lyttel oþer much be hys rewarde;
For þe gentyl Cheuentayn is no chyche,
Queþer-so-euer he dele nesch oþer harde:
He laueȝ hys gyfteȝ as water of dyche,
Oþer goteȝ of golf þat neuer charde.
Hys fraunchyse is large þat euer dard
To Hym þat matȝ in synne rescoghe;   610
No blysse betȝ fro hem reparde,
For þe grace of God is gret inoghe.

"But now, to shame me, you will state
that I took my penny wrongly here;
you say that I, who come too late,
am worthy of no reward so dear.
What man have you known to dedicate
a prayer most holy and sincere,
who never by straying from the straight
had lost the crown of heavens clear?   620
And more often with each passing year
they leave the right, to wrong they go.
Mercy and grace must then them steer,
for the grace of God is great enow.

"But enow of grace have the innocent.
When once they are born into their line,
in baptism's water they make descent;
then are they brought into the vine.
So soon they see, its light all spent,
their day to the night of death decline,   630
who never did wrong before they went.
God gives their hire, as He did mine;
they were at the work He would assign.
Why should he not their labor know
and pay what the contract did define?
For the grace of God is great enow.

"Enow is it known, without deceit,
man first was made for bliss most bright.
Our father was cast from Eden's seat;
of an apple he took a single bite.   640
We all were damned when he did eat
to die in dolor and lose delight
and thence to fall into hell's heat,
therein to dwell without respite.
But at once a remedy came in sight.
Rich blood on the rood so rough did flow,
with precious water, for our plight;
the grace of God grew great enow.

'Bot now þou moteȝ, me for to mate,
Þat I my peny haf wrang tan here;
Þou sayȝ þat I þat com to late
Am not worþy so gret fere.
Where wysteȝ þou euer any bourne abate,
Euer so holy in hys prayere,
Þat he ne forfeted by sumkyn gate
Þe mede sumtyme of heueneȝ clere?   620
And ay þe ofter, þe alder þay were,
Þay laften ryȝt and wroȝten woghe.
Mercy and grace moste hem þen stere,
For þe grace of God is gret innoȝe.

'Bot innoghe of grace hatȝ innocent.
As sone as þay arn borne, by lyne
In þe water of babtem þay dyssente:
Þen arne þay boroȝt into þe vyne.
Anon þe day, wyth derk endente,
Þe niyȝt of deth dotȝ to enclyne: 630
Þat wroȝt neuer wrang er þenne þay wente,
Þe gentyle Lorde þenne payeȝ hys hyne.
Þay dyden hys heste, þay wern þereine;
Why schulde he not her labour alow,
Ȝys, and pay hem at þe fyrst fyne?
For þe grace of God is gret innoghe.

'Inoȝe is knawen þat mankyn grete
Fyrste watȝ wroȝt to blysse parfyt;
Oure forme fader hit con forfete
Þurȝ an apple þat he vpon con byte.   640
Al wer we dampned for þat mete
To dyȝe in doel out of delyt
And syþen wende to helle hete,
Þerinne to won wythoute respyt.
Bot þeron com a bote astyt.
Ryche blod ran on rode so roghe,
And wynne water þen at þat plyt:
Þe grace of God wex gret innoghe.

"Enow then flowing from that well
of blood and water both was found.　　　　　　　　650
The blood delivered us from hell
and the second death where we were bound;
the water is baptism, truth to tell,
that dropped from the spearpoint grimly ground,
that washes away what guilts befell
when in Adam's death we all were drowned.
Now there is naught in this world round
between us and the bliss he lost, I trow;
an hour restored and made us sound,
and the grace of God is great enow.　　　　　　　660

XII

"Grace enow may the man possess
who sins anew, if he repent,
but with sorrow then he must confess
and abide what pains are consequent.
But as reason cannot from right digress,
it evermore saves the innocent;
God never judged in His righteousness
that the guiltless should bear punishment.
Through mercy is grace to the guilty sent,
if they are chastened and contrite,　　　　　　　670
but the one of no guile in intent
as an innocent is saved aright.

"Right well I know that in this case
two men will God save and sanctify;
the righteous man shall see His face,
the innocent also shall draw nigh.
In the Psalter this passage one may trace:
'Lord, who shall ascend Thy hill on high
or rest within Thy holy place?'
He is not slow to make reply:　　　　　　　　　680
'Who never on evil cast his eye
and is in heart both clean and light—
his foot is firmly fixed thereby.'
The innocent is saved by right.

'Innoghe þer wax out of þat welle,
Blod and water of brode wounde.   650
Þe blod vus boȝt fro bale of helle
And delyuered vus of þe deth secounde;
Þe water is baptem, þe soþe to telle,
Þat folȝed þe glayue so grymly grounde,
Þat wascheȝ away þe gylteȝ felle
Þat Adam wyth inne deth vus drounde.
Now is þer noȝt in þe worlde rounde
Bytwene vus and blysse bot þat he wythdroȝ,
And þat is restored in sely stounde;
And þe grace of God is gret innogh.   660

XII

'Grace innogh þe mon may haue
Þat synneȝ þenne new, ȝif hym repente,
Bot wyth sorȝ and syt he mot hit craue,
And byde þe payne þerto is bent.
Bot resoun of ryȝt þat con not raue
Saueȝ euermore þe innossent;
Hit is a dom þat neuer God gaue,
Þat euer þe gyltleȝ schulde be schente.
Þe gyltyf may contryssyoun hente
And be þurȝ mercy to grace þryȝt;   670
Bot he to gyle þat neuer glente
And inoscente is saf and ryȝte.

'Ryȝt þus I knaw wel in þis cas
Two men to saue is god by skylle:
Þe ryȝtwys man schal se hys face,
Þe harmleȝ haþel schal com hym tylle.
Þe Sauter hyt satȝ þus in a pace:
"Lorde, quo schal klymbe þy hyȝ hylle,
Oþer rest wythinne þy holy place?"
Hymself to onsware he is not dylle: 680
"Hondelyngeȝ harme þat dyt not ille,
Þat is of hert boþe clene and lyȝt,
Þer schal hys step stable stylle":
Þe innosent is ay saf by ryȝt.

"The righteous man is sure to gain
approach unto that stronghold fair,
who does not spend his life in vain
or take his neighbor in guile's snare.
For this one, Solomon did maintain,
our Wisdom a welcome must prepare;   690
He led him by ways most straight and plain
and showed him God's dominions there,
as one says, 'See! So boldly dare,
and you may win this kingdom bright.'
But assuredly, with no fear or care,
the innocent is saved by right.

"About the righteous this too is said,
in David's Psalter it may be spied:
'Lord, draw me not to Thy judgment dread;
before Thee no man is justified.'   700
When to His court you should be led,
where all our cases shall be tried,
you would be trapped if your right you pled,
as in this speech you speak in pride.
But He on the rood who bled and died,
His hands pierced through upon its height,
should let you free, when you are tried,
by innocence and not by right.

"Who rightly is able thus to read,
let him take the book to learn and see   710
how Jesus of old went forth indeed,
and many brought children to His knee,
for hap and healing from Him proceed.
That He might but touch them was their plea.
The disciples rebuked them with all speed:
'Go hence, and let the Teacher be!'
Said Jesus, 'Let them come to Me;
send not the children from My sight.
To heaven's kingdom such hold the key.'
The innocent is saved by right.   720

'The ryȝtwys man also sertayn
Aproche he schal þat proper pyle,
Þat takeȝ not her lyf in vayne,
Ne glaluereȝ her nieȝbor wyth no gyle.
Of þys ryȝtwys saȝ Salamon playn
How Koyntise onoure con aquyle;   690
By wayeȝ ful streȝt ho con hym strayn,
And scheued hym þe rengne of God awhyle,
As quo says, "Lo, ȝon louely yle!
Þou may hit wynne if þou be wyȝte."
Bot, hardyly, wythoute peryle,
Þe innosent is ay saue by ryȝte.

'Anende ryȝtwys men ȝet saytȝ a gome,
Dauid in Sauter, if euer ȝe syȝ hit:
"Lorde, Þy seruaunt draȝ neuer to dome,
For non lyuyande to þe is justyfyet."   700
Forþy to corte quen þou schal com
Þer alle oure causeȝ schal be tryed,
Alegge þe ryȝt, þou may be innome,
By þys ilke spech I haue asspyed;
Bot he on rode þat blody dyed,
Delfully þurȝ hondeȝ þryȝt,
Gyue þe to passe, when þou arte tryed,
By innocens and not by ryȝte.

'Ryȝtwysly quo con rede,
He loke on bok and be awayed   710
How Jesus hym welke in areþede,
And burneȝ her barneȝ vnto hym brayde.
For happe and hele þat fro hym ȝede
To touch her chylder þay fayr hym prayed.
His dessypeleȝ wyth blame let be hem bede
And wyth her resouneȝ ful fele restayed.
Jesus þenne hem swetely sayde:
"Do way, let chylder vnto me tyȝt.
To suche is heuenryche arayed":
Þe innocent is ay saf by ryȝt.   720

XIII

"Jesus called to Himself the mild
and said that none might His kingdom win
unless he came as though a child;
else he could never enter in.
Harmless, true, and undefiled,
without spot or stain of soiling sin,
who by the world were not beguiled—
for these, men shall the gate unpin.
There does the endless bliss begin
the jeweler sought and longed to gain;   730
he sold his goods, who rich had been,
to buy a pearl without a stain.

"This peerless pearl, in worth so dear,
for which the jeweler all did pay,
is like the realm of heaven clear—
so said the Father of brine and brae—
for it is spotless, clean, and clear,
serene and endless round for aye,
and common to all the righteous here.
Lo, even upon my breast it lay!   740
It was placed with peace, thereon to stay,
by my Lord, the Lamb who once was slain.
From this madding world now come away
and purchase your pearl without a stain."

"O stainless pearl in pearls most clean,
with the pearl of price past all compare,
who made you lovely to be seen?
With skill He wove the robe you wear.
Your beauty is not of this world's demesne;
no Pygmalion painted your face or hair,   750
nor Aristotle either, I ween,
described your nature anywhere.
Beyond fleur-de-lis is your color fair;
you seem an angel in heaven's train.
Tell me, what oyster could ever bear
this wondrous pearl without a stain?"

41

XIII

'Iesus con calle to hym hys mylde,
And sayde hys ryche no wy3 my3t wynne
Bot he com þyder ry3t as a chylde,
Oþer elle3 neuermore com þerinne.
Harmle3, trwe, and vndefylde,
Wythouten mote oþer mascle of sulpande synne,
Quen such þer cnoken on þe bylde,
Tyt schal hem men þe 3ate vnpynne.
Þer is þe blys þat con not blynne
Þat þe jueler so3te þur3 perré pres,
And solde alle hys goud, boþe wolen and lynne,
To bye hym a perle wat3 mascelle3.

'This makelle3 perle, þat bo3t is dere,
Þe joueler gef fore alle hys god,
Is lyke þe reme of heuenesse clere:
So sayde þe Fader of folde and flode;
For hit is wemle3, clene, and clere,
And endele3 rounde, and blyþe of mode,
And commune to alle þat ry3twys were.
Lo, euen inmydde3 my breste hit stode.
My Lorde þe Lombe, þat schede hys blode,
He py3t hit þere in token of pes.
I rede þe forsake þe worlde wode
And porchace þy perle maskelles.'

'O maskele3 perle in perle3 pure,
Þat bere3', quod I, 'þe perle of prys,
Quo formed þe þy fayre fygure?
Þat wro3t þy wede, he wat3 ful wys.
Þy beauté com neuer of nature;
Pymalyon paynted neuer þy vys,
Ne Arystotel nawþer by hys lettrure
Of carped þe kynde þese properté3.
Þy colour passe3 þe flour-de-lys;
Þyn angel-hauyng so clene corte3.
Breue me, bry3t, quat kyn offys
Bere3 þe perle so maskelle3?'

730

740

750

"My peerless Lamb who makes all complete,"
she said, "my own dear destiny,
chose me as His, although unmeet
that match might sometimes seem to be.   760
When I left your world's travail and heat,
He called me to joy eternally:
'Come hither to Me, my true love sweet,
for I find no spot or fault in thee.'
Power and beauty He gave to me;
in His blood He washed me in His fane
and crowned me in virginity,
adorned me in pearls without a stain."

"Why, stainless bride, with honors rife,
who shine now in the heavens bright,   770
how is it you were made the wife
of this Lamb, that He should think it right?
To lead with Him such a queenly life,
you climbed above all others in height.
So many have lived in woeful strife
for Christ's sake, with the crown in sight—
and yet you put them all to flight,
so that to this marriage none attain
except for you, so firm in might,
a peerless maid without a stain."   780

XIV

"Without a stain," said that joyful queen,
"unblemished I am, with no such blot;
so may I maintain with honor clean,
but 'peerless queen'—that said I not.
The Lamb's wives are we in bliss serene,
a hundred and forty-four thousand in lot,
as in the Apocalypse it is seen;
Saint John once saw them all in a knot.
On the hill of Zion, that lovely spot,
the apostle beheld them in a dream,   790
arrayed for the wedding on that hilltop,
the city of New Jerusalem.

'My makele3 Lambe þat al may bete',
Quod scho, 'my dere destyné,
Me ches to hys make, alþa3 vnmete
Sumtyme semed þat assemblé.   760
When I wente fro yor worlde wete,
He calde me to hys bonerté:
"Cum hyder to me, my lemman swete,
For mote ne spot is non in þe."
He gef me my3t and als bewté;
In hys blod he wesch my wede on dese,
And coronde clene in vergynté,
And py3t me in perle3 maskelle3.'

'Why, maskelle3 byrd þat bry3t con flambe,
Þat reiaté3 hat3 so ryche and ryf,   770
Quat kyn þyng may be þat Lambe
Þat þe wolde wedde vnto hys vyf?
Ouer alle oþer so hy3 þou clambe
To lede wyth hym so ladyly lyf.
So mony a comly on-vunder cambe
For Kryst han lyued in much stryf;
And þou con alle þo dere out dryf
And fro þat maryag al oþer depres,
Al only þyself so stout and styf,
A makele3 may and maskelle3.'   780

XIV

'Maskelles', quod þat myry quene,
'Vnblemyst I am, wythouten blot,
And þat may I wyth mensk menteene;
Bot "makele3 quene" þenne sade I not.
Þe Lambes vyue3 in blysse we bene,
A hondred and forty fowre þowsande flot,
As in þe Apocalyppe3 hit is sene;
Sant John hem sy3 al in a knot.
On þe hyl of Syon, þat semly clot,
Þe apostel hem segh in gostly drem   790
Arayed to þe weddyng in þat hyl-coppe,
Þe nwe cyté o Jerusalem.

44

"Of Jerusalem now in speech I spell.
If you would know of what kind is He,
my Lamb, my Lord, my jewel as well,
my joy, my bliss, my true love free,
the prophet Isaiah of Him did tell
and spoke of His humility:
'This one men would to death compel
without any charge of felony;   800
as a sheep to the slaughter led was He,
as a lamb that the shearers take is tame,
so He closed His mouth and made no plea,'
when Jews judged Him in Jerusalem.

"In Jerusalem was my true love slain
and rent on the rood by villains bold.
To bear our troubles He was fain
and took on Himself our cares so cold.
His face was bruised by blows like rain,
which had been fair once to behold.   810
For our sins He set Himself as vain,
who never had any to be told.
For us He was scourged and mocked of old
and stretched upon a sturdy beam;
as meek as a lamb to slaughter sold,
for us He died in Jerusalem.

"In Jerusalem, Jordan, and Galilee,
there good Saint John went to baptize;
his words with Isaiah did agree.
When Jesus came before his eyes,   820
he spoke of Him this prophecy:
'Behold the Lamb of God,' he cries,
'who takes away the iniquity
that over all the world now lies.'
He never sinned in any wise,
and yet to it all He made a claim.
Of His generation who testifies,
who died for us in Jerusalem?

'Of Jerusalem I in speche spelle.
If þou wyl knaw what kyn he be,
My Lombe, my Lorde, my dere juelle,
My ioy, my blys, my lemman fre,
Þe profete Ysaye of hym con melle
Pitously of hys debonerté:
"Þat gloryous gyltleȝ þat mon con quelle
Wythouten any sake of felonye,   800
As a schep to þe slaȝt þer lad watȝ he;
And, as lombe þat clypper in hande nem,
So closed he hys mouth fro vch query,
Quen Jueȝ hym iugged in Jerusalem."

'In Jerusalem watȝ my lemman slayn
And rent on rode wyth boyeȝ bolde.
Al oure baleȝ to bere ful bayn,
He toke on hymself oure careȝ colde.
Wyth boffeteȝ watȝ hys face flayn
Þat watȝ so fayr on to byholde.   810
For synne he set hymself in vayn,
Þat neuer hade non hymself to wolde.
For vus he lette hym flyȝe and folde
And brede vpon a bostwys bem;
As meke as lomp þat no playnt tolde
For vus he swalt in Jerusalem.

'In Jerusalem, Jordan, and Galalye,
Þer as baptysed þe goude Saynt Jon,
His wordeȝ acorded to Ysaye.
When Jesus con to hym warde gon.   820
He sayde of hym þys professye:
"Lo, Godeȝ Lombe as trwe as ston,
Þat dotȝ away þe synneȝ dryȝe
Þat alle þys worlde hatȝ wroȝt vpon.
Hymself ne wroȝt neuer ȝet non;
Wheþer on hymself he con al clem.
Hys generacyoun quo recen con,
Þat dyȝed for vus in Jerusalem?"

"In Jerusalem thus my love so true
twice as a lamb was counted, where   830
these faithful prophets both foreknew
the manner meek that He would bear.
The third time well accords thereto,
in Apocalypse written, which does not err.
Amid saints on thrones, His retinue,
the apostle saw Him, to declare
He opened the book with pages square,
with seven seals set on its seam;
at the sight all creatures bowed down there,
in hell, on earth, in Jerusalem.   840

XV

"This Jerusalem Lamb had never a trace
of any hue but brilliant white
that no spot or blemish may deface,
with wool in abundance, pure and bright.
Each soul that remains unstained in grace
may be to the Lamb a wife aright;
though daily they come to His embrace,
among us is no dispute or spite—
we would each be multiplied, if we might.
The more the merrier, God me bless!   850
In love does our company unite,
with honor more and never the less.

"Less of bliss none may us bring
who bear this pearl upon our breast;
they never could think of quarreling
who wear the spotless pearl as crest.
Although to clods our corpses cling
and you cry in pity with no rest,
we understand all manner of thing;
in one death all our hope we vest.   860
The Lamb gives joy; so we are blessed
whenever we feast on His largesse.
And each one's bliss is by far the best,
but still one's honor is never the less.

'In Ierusalem þus my lemman swete
Twye3 for lombe wat3 taken þare,
By trw recorde of ayþer prophete,
For mode so meke and al hys fare.
Þe þryde tyme is þerto ful mete,
In Apokalype3 wryten ful 3are;
Inmyde3 þe trone, þere saynte3 sete,
Þe apostel Iohn hym sa3 as bare,
Lesande þe boke with leue3 sware
Þere seuen syngnette3 wern sette in seme;
And at þat sy3t vche douth con dare
In helle, in erþe, and Jerusalem.

XV

'Thys Jerusalem Lombe hade neuer pechche
Of oþer huee bot quyt jolyf
Þat mot ne masklle mo3t on streche,
For wolle quyte so ronk and ryf.
Forþy vche saule þat hade neuer teche
Is to þat Lombe a worthyly wyf;
And þa3 vch day a store he feche,
Among vus comme3 nouþer strot ne stryf;
Bot vchon enlé we wolde were fyf —
Þe mo þe myryer, so God me blesse.
In compayny gret our luf con þryf
In honour more and neuer þe lesse.

'Lasse of blysse may non vus bryng
Þat beren þys perle vpon oure bereste,
For þay of mote couþe neuer mynge
Of spotle3 perle3 þat beren þe creste.
Alþa3 oure corses in clotte3 clynge,
And 3e remen for rauþe wythouten reste,
We þur3outly hauen cnawyng;
Of on dethe ful oure hope is drest.
Þe Lombe vus glade3, oure care is kest;
He myrþe3 vus alle at vch a mes.
Vchone3 blysse is breme and beste,
And neuer one3 honour 3et neuer þe les.

830

840

850

860

"Lest false you believe what I have said,
in Apocalypse it was written so:
'I see the Lamb whose blood was shed,
on the Mount of Zion, fair to show,
and with Him maidens one hundred
and four and forty thousand go.   870
I found there written on each forehead
the name of the Lamb, of God also.
Then I heard a cry from heaven grow,
as waters in a torrent press,
and as thunder rolls when stormclouds blow,
that noise, I believe, was never the less.

"'Nevertheless, though loud it brays
in a din of voices on my ear,
a note full new I heard them raise;
such dear delight it was to hear.   880
As on the harp a harper plays,
they sang that song with voices clear,
a lovely discourse of their praise.
Sweet melodies they made in fere,
at the throne of God where they appear,
and the four beasts who their Lord confess
and the solemn elders who sat near—
their song they sang then never the less.

"'Nevertheless, none has such art,
for all the crafts that ever he knew,   890
that of that song he might sing a part,
save who follow the Lamb in retinue;
for they are redeemed, from the earth apart,
as firstfruits that to God are due,
and joined to the gentle Lamb in heart
and like to Him in their face and hue.
For never falsehood or tale untrue
has touched their tongues for any distress.
That stainless host to the Master drew,
to be bound together never the less.'"   900

'Lest les þou leue my tale farande,
In Appocalyppece is wryten in wro:
"I seghe", says John, "þe Loumbe hym stande
On þe mount of Syon ful þryuen and þro,
And wyth hym maydenneʒ and hundreþe þowsande,
And fowre and forty þowsande mo.
On alle her forhedeʒ wryten I fande
Þe Lombeʒ nome, hys Fadereʒ also.
A hue from heuen I herde þoo,
Lyk flodeʒ fele laden runnen on resse,
And as þunder þroweʒ in torreʒ blo,
Þat lote, I leue, watʒ neuer þe les.

'"Nauþeles, þaʒ hit schowted scharpe,
And ledden loude alþaʒ hit were,
A note ful nwe I herde hem warpe,
To lysten þat watʒ ful lufly dere.
As harporeʒ harpen in her harpe,
Þat nwe songe þay songen ful cler,
In sounande noteʒ a gentyl carpe;
Ful fayre þe modeʒ þay fonge in fere.
Ryʒt byfore Godeʒ chayere
And þe fowre besteʒ þat hym obes
And þe aldermen so sadde of chere,
Her songe þay songen neuer þe les.

'"Nowþelese non watʒ neuer so quoynt,
For alle þe crafteʒ þat euer þay knewe,
Þat of þat songe myʒt synge a poynt,
Bot þat meyny þe Lombe þat swe;
For þay arn boʒt fro þe vrþe aloynte
As newe fryt to God ful due,
And to þe gentyl Lombe hit arn anioynt,
As lyk to hymself of lote and hwe;
For neuer lesyng ne tale vntrwe
Ne towched her tonge for no dysstresse.
Þat moteles meyny may neuer remwe
Fro þat maskeleʒ mayster, neuer þe les."'

870

880

890

900

"Never the less may you suppose
my gratitude, though doubts I bore.
My pearl, whom Christ for marriage chose,
your wit I dare to try no more.
You are so rich and rare a rose,
and I but dust, in all things poor.
In you no sin nor guile grows,
who bide here by this blissful shore
with all the joys of life in store.
Yet one thing I would ask express;   910
though churlishly I must implore,
let me prevail now never the less.

XVI

"Nevertheless on you I call,
if you may answer my behest;
as you are glorious, fair in all,
with pity grant what I request.
Have you no homes in a castle's hall,
no manor fit for each queenly guest?
You tell of Jerusalem's royal wall
that David on his throne possessed;   920
in these woods it is not found to rest,
but in Judea, that noble plot.
As under moon you are pure to test,
your dwellings should be without a spot.

"This spotless crowd of which you tell,
of thousands thronged, so great a rout—
a city great, wherein to dwell,
you must possess, I have no doubt.
For such jewels, it would not be well
if they were left to lie without,   930
and by the river in this dell
I see no building here about.
You linger alone and walk throughout
the woods to see this stream, I wot.
If you have other castles stout,
now lead me to that joyous spot."

'Neuer þe les let be my þonc',
Quod I, 'My perle, þaȝ I appose;
I schulde not tempte þy wyt so wlonc,
To Krysteȝ chambre þat art ichose.
I am bot mokke and mul among,
And þou so ryche a reken rose,
And bydeȝ here by þys blysful bonc
Þer lyueȝ lyste may neuer lose.
Now, hynde, þat sympelnesse coneȝ enclose,
I wolde þe aske a þynge expresse,
And þaȝ I be bustwys as a blose,
Let my bone vayl neuerþelese.

XVI

'Neuerþelese cler I yow bycalle,
If ȝe con se hyt be to done;
As þou art gloryous wythouten galle,
Wythnay þou neuer my ruful bone.
Haf ȝe no woneȝ in castel-walle,
Ne maner þer ȝe may mete and won?
Þou telleȝ me of Jerusalem þe ryche ryalle,
Þer Dauid dere watȝ dyȝt on trone,
Bot by þyse holteȝ hit con not hone,
Bot in Judee hit is, þat noble note.
As ȝe ar maskeleȝ vnder mone,
Your woneȝ schulde be wythouten mote.

'Þys moteleȝ meyny þou coneȝ of mele,
Of þousandeȝ þryȝt so gret a route,
A gret ceté, for ȝe arn fele,
Yow byhod haue, wythouten doute.
So cumly a pakke of joly juele
Wer euel don schulde lyȝ þeroute,
And by þyse bonkeȝ þer I con gele
I se no bygyng nawhere aboute.
I trowe alone ȝe lenge and loute
To loke on þe glory of þys gracious gote.
If þou hatȝ oþer bygyngeȝ stoute,
Now tech me to þat myry mote.'

910

920

930

"That spot you mean in Judea's land,"
then said to me that matchless maid,
"is the city where the Lamb had planned
to suffer sore for mankind's aid—   940
the old Jerusalem, to understand,
where of the old guilt an end was made.
But the new, which descended from God's hand,
the apostle as his theme essayed.
The Lamb upon whom no stain is laid
has carried thither this holy lot;
as His flock without blemish is displayed,
so is His court without a spot.

"Of two spots I speak that may be seen,
both called Jerusalem, it is true;   950
so "City of God" that name may mean,
or "Sight of Peace," which is the new—
in one was our peace secured, I ween.
The Lamb there for our sins they slew.
In the other is naught but peace to glean,
which lasts the endless ages through.
That is the city we hasten to
when our flesh is laid in earth to rot;
there bliss and glory shall accrue
to that company without a spot."   960

"Spotless maid, so meek and fair,"
I said then to that lovely flower,
"now bring me to your dwelling there
and let me see your blissful bower."
That bright one said, "In that you err!
God would forbid you from His tower,
but the Lamb has granted me this prayer,
that you shall see my royal dower.
You may look upon it for an hour
but come no nearer, not a jot;   970
to walk there you would have no power
unless you were clean without a spot.

'That mote þou meneȝ in Judy londe',
Þat specyal spyce þen to me spakk,
'Þat is þe cyté þat þe Lombe con fonde
To soffer inne sor for maneȝ sake,
Þe olde Jerusalem to vnderstonde;
For þere þe olde gulte watȝ don to slake.
Bot þe nwe, þat lyȝt of Godeȝ sonde,
Þe apostel in Apocalyppce in theme con take.
Þe Lompe þer wythouten spotteȝ blake
Hatȝ feryed þyder hys fayre flote;
And as hys flok is wythouten flake,
So is hys mote wythouten moote.

'Of motes two to carpe clene,
And Jerusalem hyȝt boþe nawþeles —
Þat nys to yow no more to mene
Bot "ceté of God", oþer "syȝt of pes":
In þat on oure pes watȝ mad at ene;
Wyth payne to suffer þe Lombe hit chese;
In þat oþer is noȝt bot pes to glene
Þat ay schal laste wythouten reles.
Þat is þe borȝ þat we to pres
Fro þat oure flesch be layd to rote,
Þer glory and blysse schal euer encres
To þe meyny þat is wythouten mote.'

'Moteleȝ may so meke and mylde',
Þen sayde I to þat lufly flor,
'Bryng me to þat bygly bylde
And let me se þy blysful bor.'
Þat schene sayde: 'Þat God wyl schylde;
Þou may not enter wythinne hys tor,
Bot of þe Lombe I haue þe aquylde
For a syȝt þerof þurȝ gret fauor.
Vtwyth to se þat clene cloystor
Þou may, bot inwyth not a fote;
To strech in þe strete þou hatȝ no vygour,
Bot þou wer clene wythouten mote.

940

950

960

970

XVII

"This spot I show and shall not hide;
go upward toward this river's head
while I follow on the other side,
until to a hill you will be led."
So then I would no longer bide
but stole through boughs with stealthy tread,
until on a hill this I espied
and gazed on the city there outspread. 980
Beyond the brook, such light it shed;
brighter than sun its glory shone.
In Apocalypse thus its form is said
to be by the apostle John.

As John the apostle saw the sight,
I saw that city so renowned,
the New Jerusalem, richly dight,
descended from heaven on that mound.
The city was all of pure gold bright,
as glass to gleaming luster ground, 990
and with the choicest gems alight.
Twelve bases its foundation crowned,
twelve levels joined with tenons sound;
each tier was made a single stone.
On this same city did expound,
in Apocalypse, the apostle John.

As John wrote every jewel's name,
I knew them from his prophecy:
the jasper was the first that came
on the fundament for me to see, 1000
on the lowest grade, in green aflame.
Of sapphire was the next degree;
translucent, with no flaw to blame,
in the third tier gleamed chalcedony.
The emerald, fourth, cut brilliantly;
the fifth was the sardonyx stone,
and the sixth, the ruby, did he see
in Apocalypse, the apostle John.

XVII

'If I þis mote þe schal vnhyde,
Bow vp towarde þys borneȝ heued,
And I anendeȝ þe on þis syde
Schal sve, tyl þou to a hil be veued.'
Þen wolde I no lenger byde,
Bot lurked by launceȝ so lufly leued,
Tyl on a hyl þat I asspyed
And blusched on þe burghe, as I forth dreued,   980
Byȝonde þe brok fro me warde keued,
Þat schyrrer þen sunne wyth schafteȝ schon.
In þe Apokalypce is þe fasoun preued,
As deuyseȝ hit þe apostel Jhon.

As John þe apostel hit syȝ wyth syȝt,
I syȝe þat cyty of gret renoun,
Jerusalem so nwe and ryally dyȝt,
As hit was lyȝt fro þe heuen adoun.
Þe borȝ watȝ al of brende golde bryȝt
As glemande glas burnist broun,   990
Wyth gentyl gemmeȝ an-vnder pyȝt
Wyth banteleȝ twelue on basyng boun,
Þe foundementeȝ twelue of riche tenoun;
Vch tabelment watȝ a serlypeȝ ston;
As derely deuyseȝ þis ilk toun
In Apocalyppeȝ þe apostel John.

As John þise stoneȝ in writ con nemme,
I knew þe name after his tale:
Jasper hyȝt þe fyrst gemme
Þat I on þe fyrst basse con wale: 1000
He glente grene in þe lowest hemme;
Saffer helde þe secounde stale;
Þe calsydoyne þenne wythouten wemme
In þe þryd table con purly pale;
Þe emerade þe furþe so grene of scale;
Þe sardonyse þe fyfþe ston;
Þe sexte þe rybé he con hit wale
In þe Apocalyppce, þe apostel John.

To these John joined the chrysolite
as seventh in the fundament;   1010
the eighth, the beryl clear and white,
beside the twin-hued topaz pent.
The chrysophrase the tenth was hight,
the jacinth as eleventh went;
the twelfth, the truest and most bright,
was amethyst, blue and purple blent.
The wall above these bases bent
was jasper that as pure glass shone;
I knew it by his testament
in Apocalpyse, the apostle John.   1020

As John described, it met my eye;
those levels twelve rose like a stair.
As long and broad as it was high,
the city above was made a square;
as clear as glass the gold streets lie,
the wall of jasper rich and rare,
the dwellings ornamented by
all kinds of gems that might be there.
The squares of that great city share
twelve furlongs' space, and so were known   1030
its height and breadth and length then, where
it was measured for the apostle John.

XVIII

As John writes, more appears to me;
the city was builded with twelve gates;
upon each side I counted three.
They were adorned with golden plates,
and each was fashioned skillfully
of a pearl whose glory never abates.
There were the names inscribed to see
of Israel's children, from their dates—   1040
that is to say, their births' estates.
The eldest was always first thereon.
In those streets such light radiates,
they needed neither sun nor moon.

Ʒet joyned John þe crysolyt
Þe seuenþe gemme in fundament;
Þe aʒtþe þe beryl cler and quyt;
Þe topasye twynne-hew þe nente endent;
Þe crysopase þe tenþe is tyʒt;
Þe jacynght þe enleuenþe gent;
Þe twelfþe, þe gentyleste in vch a plyt,
Þe amatyst purpre wyth ynde blente;
Þe wal abof þe bantels bent
O jasporye, as glas þat glysnande schon;
I knew hit by his deuysement
In þe Apocalyppeʒ, þe apostel John.

As John deuysed ʒet saʒ I þare:
Þise twelue degres wern brode and stayre;
Þe cyté stod abof ful sware,
As longe as brode as hyʒe ful fayre;
Þe streteʒ of golde as glasse al bare,
Þe wal of jasper þat glent as glayre;
Þe woneʒ wythinne enurned ware
Wyth alle kynneʒ perré þat moʒt repayre.
Þenne helde vch sware of þis manayre
Twelue forlonge space, er euer hit fon,
Of heʒt, of brede, of lenþe to cayre,
For meten hit syʒ þe apostel John.

XVIII

As John hym wryteʒ ʒet more I syʒe:
Vch pane of þat place had þre ʒateʒ;
So twelue in poursent I con asspye,
Þe portaleʒ pyked of rych plateʒ,
And vch ʒate of a margyrye,
A parfyt perle þat neuer fateʒ.
Vchon in scrypture a name con plye
Of Israel barneʒ, folewande her dateʒ,
Þat is to say, as her byrþ-whateʒ:
Þe aldest ay fyrst þeron watʒ done.
Such lyʒt þer lemed in alle þe strateʒ
Hem nedde nawþer sunne ne mone.

1010

1020

1030

1040

Of sun nor moon they needed aught;
the Lord God was their lamp for light,
the Lamb their lantern, as is taught;
through Him the city shone most bright.
Through walls and dwellings my gaze sought,
for all were clear, none hindered sight. 1050
And there a lofty throne was wrought,
with all its ornaments bedight,
as John the apostle wrote aright,
that God Himself did sit upon.
A river ran beneath its height,
more bright than either sun or moon.

Sun nor moon shone never so sweet
as the flood flowing from that base;
swiftly it rushed through every street,
of mud or mire had no trace. 1060
In the city there was no church's seat,
no chapel or temple in any space;
the Almighty made their praise complete,
the Lamb was the sacrifice of grace.
No bars or locks the gates did brace,
but ever wide open they were thrown;
none may take refuge in that place
who bears any spot beneath the moon.

From there the moon may steal no might;
too marred is she, too dull her sphere, 1070
and also there it is never night.
Why should she climb her circle here
in contest with that noble light
that shines upon the river clear?
The planets' glory is too slight,
and the sun itself too dim and blear.
About that water, trees appear
that with twelve fruits of life are strewn;
twelve times they bear them in a year
and are renewed with every moon. 1080

Of sunne ne mone had þay no nede;
Þe self God watჳ her lombe-lyჳt,
Þe Lombe her lantyrne, wythouten drede;
Þurჳ hym blysned þe borჳ al bryჳt.
Þurჳ woჳe and won my lokyng ჳede,
For sotyle cler noჳt lette no lyჳt.   1050
Þe hyჳe trone þer moჳt ჳe hede
Wyth alle þe apparaylmente vmbepyჳte,
As John þe appostel in termeჳ tyჳte;
Þe hyჳe Godeჳ self hit set vpone.
A reuer of þe trone þer ran outryჳte
Watჳ bryჳter þen boþe þe sunne and mone.

Sunne ne mone schon neuer so swete
As þat foysoun flode out of þat flet;
Swyþe hit swange þurჳ vch a strete
Wythouten fylþe oþer galle oþer glet.   1060
Kyrk þerinne watჳ non ჳete,
Chapel ne temple þat euer watჳ set;
Þe Almyჳty watჳ her mynster mete,
Þe Lombe þe sakerfyse þer to refet.
Þe ჳateჳ stoken watჳ neuer ჳet,
Bot euermore vpen at vche a lone;
Þer entreჳ non to take reset
Þat bereჳ any spot an-vnder mone.

The mone may þerof acroche no myჳte;
To spotty ho is, of body to grym,   1070
And also þer ne is neuer nyჳt.
What schulde þe mone þer compas clym
And to euen wyth þat worþly lyჳt
Þat schyneჳ vpon þe brokeჳ brym?
Þe planeteჳ arn in to pouer a plyჳt,
And þe self sunne ful fer to dym.
Aboute þat water arn tres ful schym,
Þat twelue fryteჳ of lyf con bere ful sone;
Twelue syþeჳ on ჳer þay beren ful frym,
And renowleჳ nwe in vche a mone.   1080

Beneath the moon, man's heart would fail;
such marvels it could not endure
as when I saw that city's scale,
so wondrous all its aspects were.
I stood still as a dazzled quail,
amazement so my mind did stir;
I felt no rest and no travail,
so ravished with that radiance pure.
I daresay, with conviction sure,
had one in the body received that boon,   1090
though learned men sought for his cure,
his life would be lost beneath the moon.

XIX

Just as the mighty moon will rise
ere darkness all the day has drowned,
so suddenly in wondrous wise
a procession in those streets I found.
There came a crowd, to my surprise,
in that noble city so renowned
of virgins in the selfsame guise
in which my blissful one was gowned.   1100
In that same fashion all were crowned,
adorned in pearls and robes of white;
on each one's breast was firmly bound
the blissful pearl with great delight.

With great delight they walked in fere
on golden streets that gleamed like glass.
A hundred thousand did appear,
all in the livery of their class;
each face glowed with the gladdest cheer.
Before them the Lamb did proudly pass   1110
with garb like precious pearls so dear
and seven horns red-gold as brass.
They went to the throne naught could surpass.
Though many, they had no fray or fight,
but mild as maidens seem at mass,
so they went forth with great delight.

An-vnder mone so great merwayle
No fleschly hert ne my3t endeure,
As quen I blusched vpon þat bayle,
So ferly þerof wat3 þe fasure.
I stod as stylle as dased quayle
For ferly of þat frelich fygure,
Þat felde I nawþer reste ne trauayle,
So wat3 I rauyste wyth glymme pure.
For I dar say wyth conciens sure,
Hade bodyly burne abiden þat bone,   1090
Þa3 alle clerke3 hym hade in cure,
His lyf were loste an-vnder mone.

XIX

Ry3t as þe maynful mone con rys
Er þenne þe day-glem dryue al doun,
So sodanly on a wonder wyse
I wat3 war of a prosessyoun.
Þis noble cité of ryche enpryse
Wat3 sodanly ful wythouten sommoun
Of such vergyne3 in þe same gyse
Þat wat3 my blysful an-vnder croun: 1100
And coronde wern alle of þe same fasoun,
Depaynt in perle3 and wede3 qwyte;
In vchone3 breste wat3 bounden boun
Þe blysful perle wyth gret delyt.

Wyth gret delyt þay glod in fere
On golden gate3 þat glent as glasse;
Hundreth þowsande3 I wot þer were,
And alle in sute her liuré3 wasse;
Tor to knaw þe gladdest chere.
Þe Lombe byfore con proudly passe   1110
Wyth horne3 seuen of red golde cler;
As praysed perle3 his wede3 wasse.
Towarde þe throne þay trone a tras.
Þa3 þay wern fele, no pres in plyt,
Bot mylde as maydene3 seme at mas,
So dro3 þay forth wyth gret delyt.

The delight His coming did supply
would be too much for me to tell.
The elders bowed when He drew nigh;
prostrate before His feet they fell. 1120
Legions of angels from on high
spread incense that was sweet to smell.
The more that gem to glorify,
the louder still their song did swell.
Those strains might strike through earth to hell
when heaven's Virtues their joys recite.
To love the Lamb where His servants dwell,
truly I took a great delight.

A delight the Lamb was to my eyes;
much marvel in my mind there went. 1130
Best was He, brightest, and most to prize
of any one might in speech present;
so worthily white was all His guise,
His looks so simple in pure intent.
But a wound full wide and wet did rise
close by His heart, where the skin was rent.
His side was all with blood besprent.
Alas, thought I, who did that spite?
One's breast should burn with sad lament
ere in that he would have delight. 1140

The Lamb's delight none would doubt, I ween.
Though He was wounded with a blade,
in His countenance it was never seen;
His glance with glorious light was rayed.
I looked on His company serene,
how much of life in them was laid;
then I saw there my little queen,
who I thought stood by me in the glade.
Lord, much was the mirth she made
among her peers who shone so white! 1150
That sight made me think to cross and wade,
for longing of love in great delight.

Delyt þat hys come encroched
To much hit were of for to melle
Þise aldermen, quen he aproched,
Grouelyng to his fete þay felle.   1120
Legyounes of aungeleȝ togeder uoched
Þer kesten ensens of swete smelle.
Þen glory and gle watȝ nwe abroched;
Al songe to loue þat gay juelle.
Þe steuen moȝt stryke þurȝ þe vrþe to helle
Þat þe Vertues of heuen of joye endyte.
To loue þe Lombe his meyny in melle
Iwysse I laȝt a gret delyt.

Delit þe Lombe for to deuise
Wyth much meruayle in mynde went.   1130
Best watȝ he, blyþest, and moste to pryse,
Þat euer I herde of speche spent;
So worþly whyt wern wedeȝ hys,
His lokeȝ symple, hymself so gent.
Bot a wounde ful wyde and weete con wyse
Anende hys hert, þurȝ hyde torente.
Of his quyte syde his blod outsprent.
Alas, þoȝt I, who did þat spyt?
Ani breste for bale aȝt haf forbrent
Er he þerto hade had delyt.   1140

The Lombe delyt non lyste to wene.
Þaȝ he were hurt and wounde hade,
In his sembelaunt watȝ neuer sene,
So wern his glenteȝ gloryous glade.
I loked among his meyny schene
How þay wyth lyf wern laste and lade;
Þen saȝ I þer my lyttel quene
Þat I wende had standen by me in sclade.
Lorde, much of mirþe watȝ þat ho made
Among her fereȝ þat watȝ so quyt!   1150
Þat syȝt me gart to þenk to wade
For luf-longyng in gret delyt.

XX

Delight rushed in my eye and ear,
my mortal mind to madness hied;
when I saw my pearl, I would come near,
though beyond the water she must bide.
I thought no hindrance could appear
to keep me from the other side,
and from the stream none could me steer,
to swim it even if I died.   1160
But in that aim I was denied.
When in I would spring and go astray,
I was taken from it ere I tried;
it was against my Prince's way.

His way was not that I should cross o'er
the wondrous stream; that He forbade.
Rashly I rushed and recked no more,
but quickly then I was forestayed.
For just as I sprang upon the shore,
my dream was broken and unmade.   1170
I woke in that garden, as before;
my head upon that hill was laid
where my pearl into the ground had strayed.
Awakened, I fell in great dismay,
and sighing to myself I prayed,
"Let all be done in that Prince's way."

I rued the way that I must leave
so suddenly that region fair,
those sights so lovely to perceive.
A heavy longing struck me there,   1180
and swooning I could not but grieve;
"O pearl," said I, "renowned and rare,
how dear these words that I believe,
that in this vision you did declare!
If true and honest speech you share
who come adorned in garland gay,
I am glad, in this dungeon of despair,
that you walk in that Prince's way."

XX

Delyt me drof in y3e and ere,
My mane3 mynde to maddyng malte;
Quen I se3 my frely, I wolde be þere,
By3onde þe water þa3 ho were walte.
I þo3t þat noþyng my3t me dere
To fech me bur and take me halte,
And to start in þe strem schulde non me stere,
To swymme þe remnaunt, þa3 I þer swalte.   1160
Bot of þat munt I wat3 bitalt;
When I schulde start in þe strem astraye,
Out of þat caste I wat3 bycalt:
Hit wat3 not at my Prynce3 paye.

Hit payed hym not þat I so flonc
Ouer meruelous mere3, so mad arayde.
Of raas þa3 I were rasch and ronk,
3et rapely þerinne I wat3 restrayed.
For, ry3t as I sparred vnto þe bonc,
Þat brathþe out of my drem me brayde.   1170
Þen wakned I in þat erber wlonk;
My hede vpon þat hylle wat3 layde
Þer as my perle to grounde strayd.
I raxled, and fel in gret affray,
And, sykyng, to myself I sayd,
'Now al be to þat Prynces paye'.

Me payed ful ille to be outfleme
So sodenly of þat fayre regioun,
Fro alle þo sy3te3 so quyke and queme.
A longeyng heuy me strok in swone,   1180
And rewfully þenne I con to reme:
'O perle', quod I, 'of rych renoun,
So wat3 hit me dere þat þou con deme
In þys veray avysyoun!
If hit be ueray and soth sermoun
Þat þou so styke3 in garlande gay,
So wel is me in þys doel-doungoun
Þat þou art to þat Prynse3 paye.'

To that Prince's way I might have bent,
not yearned to be more greatly blessed,   1190
and held to that with true intent,
as prayed my pearl in beauty dressed;
toward God I might have made ascent
to move through mysteries unguessed.
But ever a man is discontent
with fortune that he has possessed.
Therefore I was rent from joy and rest;
I was cast from the land that lasts for aye.
They are mad who against You, Lord, contest
or offer You aught against Your way.   1200

The way to please the Prince aright
for the Christian is easy to divine;
for I have found Him, both day and night,
a God, a Lord, a friend most fine.
On this mound I had this wondrous sight,
for the sake of my pearl, for which I pine;
I committed it to the God of might
in Christ's dear blessing and likewise mine,
He whom in the form of bread and wine
the priest shows to us every day.   1210
He grants that we serve Him, so to shine
as precious pearls unto His way.

Amen.

To þat Prynceȝ paye hade I ay bente,
And ȝerned no more þen watȝ me gyuen,   1190
And halden me þer in trwe entent,
As þe perle me prayed þat watȝ so þryuen,
As helde, drawen to Goddeȝ present,
To mo of his mysterys I hade ben dryuen;
Bot ay wolde man of happe more hente
Þen moȝte by ryȝt vpon hem clyuen.
Þerfore my ioye watȝ sone toriuen,
And I kaste of kytheȝ þat lasteȝ aye.
Lorde, mad hit arn þat agayn þe stryuen,
Oþer proferen þe oȝt agayn þy paye.   1200

To pay þe Prince oþer sete saȝte
Hit is ful eþe to þe god Krystyin;
For I haf founden hym, boþe day and naȝte,
A God, a Lorde, a frende ful fyin.
Ouer þis hyul þis lote I laȝte,
For pyty of my perle enclyin,
And syþen to God I hit bytaȝte
In Krysteȝ dere blessyng and myn,
Þat in þe forme of bred and wyn
Þe preste vus scheweȝ vch a daye.   1210
He gef vus to be his homly hyne
Ande precious perleȝ vnto his pay.

Amen.

Notes

Notes are listed by line number. Biblical references and quotations are from the Douay–Rheims Version, the English translation of the Latin Vulgate with which the Pearl Poet would have been familiar.

3...*the Orient*...The most valuable pearls were imported from East Asia via the Mediterranean. Although by the late fourteenth century a number of merchants and missionaries had traveled in Asia and written of their experiences, most Europeans would still have thought of "the Orient" as a distant, mysterious land.

11...*lovelorn longing*...Sarah Stanbury notes that the term *luf-daungere* is a coinage derived from the vocabulary of courtly love. It evokes the power of the unattainable lady and anticipates the Pearl-Maiden's status as the queenly bride of Christ, no longer merely a child.

31...*seeds that are dead*...Cf. John 12:24-25: "Amen, amen I say to you, unless the grain of wheat falling into the ground die, itself remaineth alone. But if it die, it bringeth forth much fruit." Also cf. 1 Corinthians 15:36-38.

39...*Lammas-time*...The mention in the next line of reaping grain indicates that the "hygh seysoun" is Lammas, a festival on August 1 celebrating the wheat harvest. It has also been suggested that the holiday may be the Feast of the Assumption of the Virgin (August 15) or the Feast of the Transfiguration of Christ (August 8), either of which could relate to the Pearl-Maiden's glorification in heaven.

91...*citole or gittern*...The citole and gittern were string instruments; both are considered precursors of the modern guitar.

195...*fleur-de-lis*...The fleur-de-lis, like the botanical lily, was often associated with the Virgin Mary, symbolizing purity. It was connected to the "lily among the thorns" in Canticles 2:2, which was interpreted as a reference to Mary.

209...*No coif or wimple*...The Pearl-Maiden's unbound hair emphasizes the childlike aspect of her appearance as well as recalling medieval images of the virgin martyrs, who were usually depicted with loose hair and no headdress.

231...*from here to Greece*...A similar hyperbole is used in *Sir Gawain and the Green Knight*, line 2023: Gawain in his splendid gear is "the gayest into Grece."

259...*casket*...Like *casket*, the Middle English *cofer* has the double meaning of "a box for the storage of valuables" and "a coffin."

343...*no redress*...In the Middle English, "gains you not a cress," i.e., gains you not a straw, gets you nothing.

430...*Phoenix of Araby*...Because of its power of rebirth, the phoenix was used as a symbol of Christ's resurrection, but it could also symbolize the Immaculate Conception of the Virgin Mary.

457...*so says Saint Paul*...Cf. 1 Corinthians 12:12-31. Paul describes Christians as "members of Christ"; like the parts of the body, given different roles, but joined in what should be a harmonious whole.

472...Here a line is missing in the manuscript. In his 1891 edition, Sir Israel Gollancz supplies *Me thynk thou spekes now ful wronge.*

497...*Matthew's message*...The Parable of the Vinedressers is recounted in Matthew 20:1-16.

555...*not two hours*...In the parable, the laborers complain that the other men have worked only one hour; "houres two" recalls the Pearl-Maiden's earthly life of less than two years.

567...*turned to spite*...Cf. Matthew 20:15: "Is thy eye evil, because I am good?"

595...*Thou giv'st*...The reference here is uncertain. Possibly, cf. Psalm 61:13: "And mercy to thee, O Lord; for thou wilt render to every man according to his works."

678...*Lord, who shall ascend*...Cf. Psalm 23:3-4: "Who shall ascend into the mountain of the Lord: or who shall stand in his holy place? The innocent in hands, and clean of heart, who hath not taken his soul in vain, nor sworn deceitfully to his neighbour."

689...*Solomon did maintain*...Cf. Wisdom 10:10, in the Apocrypha: "She conducted the just, when he fled from his brother's wrath, through the right ways, and shewed him the kingdom of God..." Instead of this female personification, the poet here depicts Christ as "our Wisdom."

699...*Lord, draw me not*...Cf. Psalm 142:2: "And enter not into judgment with thy servant: for in thy sight no man living shall be justified."

715...*The disciples rebuked them*...Cf. Matthew 19:13-15, as well as Mark 10:13-16 and Luke 18:15-17.

730...*the jeweler sought*...The Parable of the Pearl of Great Price is recounted in Matthew 13:45-46. There the man is stated to be a merchant, not a jeweler.

733...*This peerless pearl*...Some editors amend *makelles* to *mascelles*, but others retain. The poet appears to be making a play on the words.

736...*brine and brae*...As a translation of "folde and flode," sea and land, i.e., the entire world.

750...*Pygmalion painted*...A reference to the Greek myth of Pygmalion, a sculptor who made a statue so beautiful that he fell in love with it. In the Middle Ages, this story was often used to portray the danger of art leading to idolatry and sometimes to depict the contrast between artifice and nature.

775...*So many*...The poet renews his objection from lines 473-480: How can the Pearl-Maiden achieve such a lofty status in heaven, when others have suffered, and presumably merited, so much more than she?

786...*a hundred and forty-four thousand*...The poet's depiction of the hundred and forty-four thousand differs substantially from the biblical account. In Revelation 7, they are stated to be from "every tribe of the children of Israel" and are marked with the seal of God. Interpretations vary; in Catholic doctrine, 144,000 is considered to be not a literal number, but a symbolic number denoting a multitude, and Israel to be the "spiritual Israel," i.e., the Church. Revelation 14:4 mentions that the hundred and forty-four thousand are virgins, but says that they "were not defiled with women," and in the Vulgate the words used to refer to them are grammatically masculine. Nowhere are they said to be female or "the Lamb's wives."

801...*as a sheep*...Cf. Isaiah 53:7: "He was offered because it was his own will, and he opened not his mouth: he shall be led as a sheep to the slaughter, and shall be dumb as a lamb before his shearer, and he shall not open his mouth."

817...*In Jerusalem*...In the Gospels, John the Baptist is recorded as ministering only in the area around the Jordan River, not in Jerusalem or Galilee.

822...*Behold the Lamb*...Cf. John 1:28-31, 35-36.

837...*He opened the book*...Cf. Revelation 5. There the "book" is a scroll, while the poet's mention of "pages square" indicates a codex.

867...*I see the Lamb*...For the imagery used in this and the following two stanzas, see Revelation 14:1-5.

886...*the four beasts*...In Revelation 4 and elsewhere, the four beasts, referred to in many translations as the "four living creatures," are angelic beings often specifically identified as cherubim. In the Middle Ages, they were also considered to represent the Four Evangelists: Mark, the lion; Luke, the ox; Matthew, the man; and John, the eagle.

887...*the solemn elders*...The twenty-four elders are generally considered to represent either the Church or the twelve tribes of Israel and twelve apostles. The poet's referring to them as "aldermen" adds an element of familiarity to the heavenly scene, as well as another analogy to earthly courts and governments.

911...*though churlishly*...Here, as in line 382, the narrator's concern is with his lack of manners and nobility as compared to the perfect courtly behavior of the Pearl-Maiden.

923...*under moon*...I.e., on the sublunary earth. For association of the moon with comparative imperfection, see also lines 1069-70, where it is said to be "to spotty" and dull beside the divine light of the New Jerusalem.

924...*without a spot*...In Middle English, *mote*, like *spot*, carries the double meaning of "place, dwelling" and "blemish."

941...*The old Jerusalem*...The Pearl-Maiden contrasts the "old" or terrestrial Jerusalem, considered the place of law, with the celestial New Jerusalem of grace made available through Christ's settlement of the "old guilt."

951...*City of God*...Both the old and new Jerusalem could be referred to as the "City of God." The name was also interpreted to mean "Sight of Peace" (*visio pacis*) from the Hebrew *shalom*.

958...*to rot*...For the Pearl-Maiden's other references to the dissolution of the dead's earthly bodies, see lines 320 and 857. The theme of bodily decomposition is prominent at the beginning of the poem, as the narrator mourns that his pearl is "marred with a dirty clot" while also praising the flowers that seem to grow from her decay.

985...*As John the apostle saw*...See Revelation 21:10-25 for the description of the New Jerusalem.

1007...*the ruby*...In the biblical account, the sixth tier is sardius or sard, a semi-precious stone similar to the carnelian.

1030...*twelve furlongs' space*...In Revelation, 12,000 furlongs; in the poem, "twelve" may be a scribal error.

1055...*A river ran*...See Revelation 22:1-2 for the river flowing from the throne and the trees of life subsequently mentioned.

1090...*in the body*...This line recalls the narrator's statement in lines 61-64 that only his spirit received the vision, while his body was left sleeping.

1108...*the livery*...The translation of *livrés* as "livery" again makes heaven analogous to an earthly court.

1112...*seven horns*...Cf. Revelation 5:6.

1126...*heaven's Virtues*...The "Virtues" are a specific order in the traditional hierarchy of angels devised in medieval theology.

1208...*in Christ's dear blessing*...This was a benediction often, although not exclusively, used in letters from parents to children.

1209...*form of bread and wine*...A conventional formula describing the Eucharist.

Glossary of Rare and Archaic Words

aye ever, always

bedight adorned, bedecked

besprent sprinkled

comely beautiful, attractive

damozel damsel, maiden, young woman

demesne domain, territory

dight adorned, arrayed

empery empire, dominion

enow enough

fain willing

fane temple, sacred place

fay faith; *in fay, by my fay* in faith, by my faith

fere companion; *in fere* together, in company

forestay to forestall, prevent

gillyvor gillyflower; the clove pink or carnation

hap fortune, especially good fortune

hie to hurry, go quickly

hight called, named

ken to know, see, perceive

lea field, meadow

lief dear, beloved

may maiden

plain to lament

plight plait, braid

ply to work diligently

reck to care, heed

rood the cross on which Christ was crucified

spell to speak, tell

trow to believe, trust

twain to part, divide

unmeet unfitting

vinery vineyard

weal a state of well-being

ween to think, believe, suppose

wight being, person

wise way, manner; *in any wise* in any way

wot from *wit*, to know